MW01026362

THE ALLURE
OF GENTLENESS

Also by Dallas Willard

THE ALLURE
OF GENTLENESS

Defending the Faith in the Manner of Jesus

DALLAS WILLARD

HarperOne
An Imprint of HarperCollins*Publishers*

HarperOne

THE ALLURE OF GENTLENESS: *Defending the Faith in the Manner of Jesus.*

HarperCollins books may be purchased for educational, business, or sales promotional use. For information please email the Special Markets Department at SPsales@harpercollins.com.

HarperCollins website: http://www.harpercollins.com

HarperCollins®, ®, and HarperOne™ are trademarks of HarperCollins Publishers.

FIRST EDITION

Library of Congress Cataloging-in-Publication Data

Willard, Dallas.
  The allure of gentleness : defending the faith in the manner of Jesus / Dallas Willard. — First edition.
      pages   cm
  ISBN 978-0-06-211408-2
  1. Apologetics. I. Title.
  BT1103.W544   2015
  239—dc23   2014035607

15 16 17 18 19   RRD(H)   10 9 8 7 6 5 4 3 2 1

CONTENTS

For Larissa Raphael Heatley,
the apple of her Grandpa's eye
and a beautiful example of
how to gently love people
into the kingdom of God.

PREFACE

What are the hard questions that smother faith?

—DALLAS WILLARD

The question above comes from a conversation I had with my father, Dallas Willard, about this book. Answering hard questions is what he wanted the book to do. In other discussions, he articulated the spirit he wanted it to have: "Gentleness: Apologetics in the Manner of Jesus." Not a gentleness marked by passivity, but a gentleness aglow with shoulder-to-shoulder journeying together over steep hills and through dark valleys. He wanted this book to help people wrestle with common doubts and answer some of the hard questions, allowing more room for the Spirit to advance their faith.

Gentle was a word frequently used to describe my father; he had a gentleness that seemed to come from his many years in the light and easy yoke of Christ. Is gentleness an absence of power or a power born through the Spirit and found in wisdom? Matthew 12:20 says Jesus would not even break a bruised reed or quench a smoldering wick, and yet his gentleness launched a worldwide revolution. In many ways, Jesus's impact seems to be not in spite of his gentleness, but because of it.

Today apologetics has become something of a cage match revolving around proofs of God's existence and involvement in the world. It has become a harsh battleground for the intelligent design-versus-Darwinism debate and other hot-button religion-versus-science arguments. What's lost in today's "apologetics" is to gently and lovingly address—even *welcome*—the honest doubts and questions that burden believers' faith.

> But the wisdom from above is first pure, then peaceable, gentle, willing to yield, full of mercy and good fruits, without a trace of partiality or hypocrisy. (James 3:17)

In the same way that *The Divine Conspiracy* addressed discipleship as the hole in our conception of the gospel Jesus preached, my father and I hoped this book would help return the field of apologetics to its wise and gentle roots.

This book began as a four-part series of talks given by my father in 1990 at Grace Church in Los Alamitos, California. As I listened to the cassette tapes a few years ago, I was impressed with the uniqueness of this teaching—particularly regarding the manner with which we should approach apologetics. I asked my dad if he would consider letting me transcribe the talks, so that they could be published as a book. He immediately agreed, with the stipulation that he would make additions to the text to be sure that all the important topics were included.

Before we were able to work on those additional topics, my father began struggling with health issues and was eventually diagnosed with cancer. For many months he told me, "Don't do anything with the book yet. We'll work on it when I'm feeling better." At the time of his passing, I still just had the list of additions he wanted to make, with various notes on specific topics.

Thankfully, he left us with papers and recordings that covered everything on the list. The Grace Church series provided significant content, forming the outline and progression of the book (you can listen to the audio version at www.dwillard .org), while notes from a similar series presented at Los Angeles Baptist College and notes for a course on Biblical Apologetics at the Simon Greenleaf School of Law provided excellent reference material to expand on that teaching. A few of my father's papers and articles written for other occasions filled in some of his additional topics. This includes a very important paper entitled "Pain, the Existence of God, and Related Problems," which is the primary source for the chapter on evil.

I am particularly indebted to the late Frank Pastore, of KKLA Radio in Los Angeles, and John Ortberg, of Menlo Park Presbyterian Church, both of whom interviewed Dallas on numerous occasions and asked the hard questions about life and faith. Segments from recordings of those interviews provided additional content on specific topics throughout the book.

In bringing these pieces together, I felt like a tailor who has been blessed with a bolt of beautiful cloth and a perfect pattern. The fabric and pattern come entirely from Dallas; only the stitching is mine. My prayer is that I have sewn this together in such a way that the stitching doesn't show and that my father's thoughts and ideas are all that is seen. May this book help us do as he prayed: "To be simple, humble, and thoughtful as we listen to others and help them come to faith in the One who has given us life."

—*Rebecca Willard Heatley*
June 2014

INTRODUCTION

When most people who are familiar with it hear the word *apologetics,* they likely associate it with words like *argument, evidence, reason,* or *defense.*[1] But few would think to add *gentle* or *gentleness* to the list.

That is because the word *apologetics* came to us from the Greek legal system, where one makes one's *defense* against the prosecutor's charges. That is not the ideal context for gentleness. But the apostle Paul and other New Testament writers adapted this term, so that apologetics came to describe Christian attempts to *defend* or *explain* the faith to others. And this is how the church has come to use the term.

For example, since the four Gospels were written to make the case for who Jesus was and what he accomplished and taught, their authors are called *apologists,* as are those today who specialize in defending Christianity against its critics. Since the time of the great debates surrounding the rise of science and rationalism and the corollary attacks on the church's commitment to the supernatural, apologetics has become increasingly preoccupied with intellectual debates and arguments.

Now, in principle, there is nothing wrong with this. Since apologetics is involved with ideas, intellectual claims, and reasoning, it is fitting for apologists to engage in intellectual debates and arguments. However, as we will see in this book, given we are seeking to do apologetics in the manner of Jesus, what is not fitting is for apologists to engage in debates and arguments with an antagonizing, arrogant spirit. Indeed, the best way to make the intellectual aspects of apologetics more effective is to combine them with a gentle spirit and kind presentation.

When we do the work of apologetics, we do it as disciples of Jesus—and therefore we are to do it in the manner in which he would do it. This means, above all, that we do it to help people, and especially those who *want* to be helped. That is how all of Jesus's work is characterized in scripture. Apologetics is a helping ministry.

The picture presented in the context of 1 Peter 3:8-17 is that of disciples who are devoted to promoting what is good, but who are being persecuted for it. Their response, as Jesus had taught them, was to "rejoice and be glad" (Matt. 5:12). This led those looking on to inquire how the disciples could be joyous and hopeful in such circumstances. The question would, of course, be inevitable in an angry, hopeless, and joyless world. So the disciples were charged by Peter: "Be ready to make your defense to anyone who demands from you an accounting for the hope that is in you; yet do it with gentleness and reverence. Keep your conscience clear" (1 Pet. 3:15–16).

As we give our explanation, our apologetic, as an act of neighbor love with "gentleness and reverence," Jesus tells us we are to be "as shrewd as serpents" and "as innocent as doves" (Matt. 10:16, NIV). The serpent's wisdom, shrewdness, is timeliness based on watchful observation. And doves are innocent in that they are incapable of guile or of misleading anyone. So are we to be. Love of those we deal with will help us to observe them accurately and refrain from manipulating them—at the same time that we intensely long and pray for them to recognize that Jesus Christ is master of the cosmos in which they live.

What does it mean that we are to be characterized by gentleness? To begin with, it means being humble. Love will purge us of any desire merely to win as well as of intellectual self-righteousness and contempt for the opinions and abilities of others. The apologist for Christ is one characterized by "humbleness of mind" (tapeinophrosunen;[2] Col. 3:12; Acts 20:19; 1 Pet. 5:5)—a vital New Testament concept that cannot be captured by our word "humility" alone.

So the call to "give an account" is, first, not a call to beat unwilling people into intellectual submission, but to be the servant of those in need, often indeed the servant of those who are in the grip of their own intellectual self-righteousness and pride, usually reinforced by their social surroundings.

Second, we do the work of apologetics as relentless servants of truth. Jesus said that he "came into the world to testify to the truth" (John 18:37), and he is called "the faithful and true witness" (Rev. 3:14). This is why we give our account with reverence (or fear, KJV). Truth reveals reality, and reality can be described as what we humans run into when we are wrong, a collision in which we always lose.

Being mistaken about life, the things of God, and the human soul is a deadly serious matter. That is why the work of apologetics is so important. So we speak the truth in love (Eph. 4:15). And we speak with all the clarity and reasonableness we can muster, simultaneously counting on the Spirit of truth (John 16:13) to accomplish, with what we do, an effect that lies far beyond our natural abilities.

Finding real truth is the point of reference we share with all human beings. No one can live without truth. Though we may disagree about which particular things are true or false, allegiance to truth—whatever the truth may be—permits us to stand alongside every person as honest fellow inquirers. Our attitude is therefore not one of "us and them," but of "we." And we are forever here to learn together, not only to teach.

So, if at all possible—sometimes it is not, due to others—we "give our account" in an atmosphere of mutual inquiry animated by generous love. However firm we may be in our convictions, we do not become overbearing, contemptuous, hostile, or defensive. We know that Jesus himself would not do so, because we cannot help people in that way. He had no need of it, nor do we. And in apologetics, as everywhere, he is our model and our master. Our confidence is totally in him. That is the "special place" we give him in our hearts—how we "in [our] hearts sanctify Christ as Lord" (1 Pet. 3:15)—in the crucial service of apologetics.

And that is why our apologetic needs to be characterized by gentleness. Like Jesus, we are reaching out in love in a humble spirit with no coercion. The only way to accomplish that is to present our defense gently, as help offered in love in the manner of Jesus.

But that is not all. The means of our communication needs to be gentle, because gentleness also characterizes the subject of our communication. What we are seeking to defend or explain is Jesus himself, who is a gentle, loving shepherd. If we are not gentle in how we present the good news, how will people encounter the gentle and loving Messiah we want to point to?

And finally, in an age shaped by feuding intellectual commitments and cultural battles over religion, science, truth, and morality, how will we get a hearing by merely insisting that we have truth and reason on our side? Many have made these claims before us. Some in a spirit of aggression, some in fear, and some in arrogance. Our apologetic happens in a context, and that context is strewn with enmity, hostility, abuse, and other opposition, which ultimately contradict the very things our message lifts up. That is why our apologetic has to embody the message and person we want to communicate. Only with "gentleness and reverence" will people be able to see, verify, and be persuaded to respond to what we have to say.

In the rest of this book I will cover many important topics concerned with what it means to defend the faith in the twenty-first century, including the role of the Bible, ethics, philosophy, the history of ideas, and so on. But it will all be wasted unless the allure of gentleness pervades all that we do.

Chapter One

BEGINNING TO THINK FOR CHRIST

And this is my prayer, that your love may overflow more and more with knowledge and full insight to help you to determine what is best, so that in the day of Christ you may be pure and blameless, having produced the harvest of righteousness that comes through Jesus Christ for the glory and praise of God.

PHILIPPIANS 1:9–11

For this reason, since the day we heard it, we have not ceased praying for you and asking that you may be filled with the knowledge of God's will in all spiritual wisdom and understanding, so that you may lead lives worthy of the Lord, fully pleasing to him, as you bear fruit in every good work and as you grow in the knowledge of God.

COLOSSIANS 1:9–10

A pologetics is a New Testament ministry that uses thinking and reasoning, in reliance on the Holy Spirit, to assist earnest inquirers in relinquishing disbelief and mistrust in God and God's good purposes for humankind. Apologetic work helps people believe and know the things that are especially related to Jesus Christ: his coming into the world, his life and death, and now his continuing to live in us. Apologetics is a vital ministry of the New Testament.

Today *apologetics* is a rather foreboding word. If you say to your neighbors, "I'm going to do apologetics with you," they would probably run away and hide. But what we're really talking about is aiding others in removing doubts that hinder their enthusiastic and full participation in the kingdom of the heavens[1] and their discipleship to Christ. We have many clear indications in scripture that we are intended to add to our faith: that we start with faith, but we move on to knowledge; that we are to grow not only in grace, but also in the knowledge of our Lord and Savior, Jesus Christ (2 Pet. 1:5; 3:18).

There's nothing wrong with faith. Faith is a confidence or trust in something, which we may or may not know to be true. But one of the things we need to keep in mind about faith is that it may be wrong. Sometimes we trust and have confidence in things that betray us, because they are false. Christians are not the only ones who live by faith. Everyone lives and dies by faith. Faith in itself is not necessarily a good or a bad thing. Now, there is a saving faith, and that's a good thing. But there are damning faiths as well. And there are also the situations where we live neither in knowledge nor in faith; we're just in doubt. These are situations that Jesus dealt with often, and we want to learn to have his spirit in dealing with doubt. (A good example of his methodology is found in his conversation with the Samaritan woman at the well in John 4.)

Faith is not opposed to evidence that we might gain from perception as well as from reason. Anything that we can use to remove and settle doubt that afflicts us or others around us is good. God has given us natural abilities, and it is right and good to devote them to God.

The intellect is good. Our natural abilities of perception are good, and they are not opposed to faith. Please hear me: our natural abilities are not opposed to faith. Yes, we live by faith and not by sight, but try not using your sight at all and see how that works. When Jesus walked this earth, he used *all* of his human powers—all of them—and we are called to devote *all* of our human powers to God in order that we might live under him as he intended.

So we use our natural reason, under the guidance and power of the Holy Spirit, in the work of apologetics to bring information and logic to bear on doubts that prevent a steady, clear perception of the realities of God's kingdom.

HIDING FROM GOD

People can also use their reason to hide from God, and he will cooperate with them (up to a point). God has so ordained that if we wish to hide from him, he will hide from us. He has created the world and arranged history so that human beings can have a way to avoid him, but also so that they can find him in their own way. Many people wonder about this arrangement, and I will go over it carefully in Chapter 6.

You may remember the old "village atheist" trick of putting a watch on the podium and saying, "Now, if there is a God, in five minutes he must strike me dead." Not a single person who has given that challenge has ever received a response. This whole routine is a piece of Americana that may be on the verge of being forgotten. People like the nineteenth-century orator Bob Ingersoll and others used to go across the country and try to bait churches with this kind of thing. As if that was really proof! It's the equivalent of an ant walking through your room and saying, "If there is a person up there reading a book, in five minutes he will throw the book down on me." Well, you've got more important things to do than throw this book at an ant! And after all, if you wanted to approach ants, one of the things you *wouldn't* do is go around throwing books at them. This is just one example of the little tricks based on assumptions about the nature of God that are totally wrong. And in truth, the people who are pulling tricks like this don't *want* to find God, and they don't want you to find him either.

Another way people hide from God is through idea systems. Let me tell you about one idea system that Christians need to address. It's the idea that we *just have faith* in the church, but we don't *know* anything. It's the idea that knowledge is *opposed* to faith. People know things over in the shopping center, they know things at the bank, and they know things at school. But when you come to church, there is no knowledge, just faith.

You may have a hard time believing that, but if you want to understand why the Christian gospel is being treated in this country as it is now by those running the legal and school systems, you have to realize that they have been trained by a system of ideas to believe that Christianity is *just another superstition*—one, moreover, that has had a legal advantage in this country and should now be dispossessed of that legal advantage. This is very deeply ingrained in the idea system that governs life around us.

Many Christians, in their heart of hearts, also believe that their faith is just another superstition. They really do. That is why I often say that I know many people who believe in Jesus, but don't believe in God. I may say a number of things in this book that I hope you will worry about, really. You see, I don't live with the assumption that I am right about everything, but I do live with the assumption that we should earnestly inquire and use our minds together under God to seek understanding.

I encourage you to do your own study on what scripture says about knowledge as opposed to faith. Go to www.biblegateway .com, search the word *know,* and compare it to *belief* and *faith.* I think you are going to be tremendously surprised at the place of knowledge in following Christ.

WHAT IS KNOWLEDGE?

We need a good understanding of what knowledge is and how it works, because one of the greatest issues facing the church is whether we have *knowledge* or just *belief*. When you believe something, you are ready to act as if it were so when the circumstances are appropriate.

Now, it's also important to distinguish belief from commitment here. You may be committed to something even though you don't believe it. We see this in sports all the time. The fans keep cheering for their team—when they are behind by thirty points and there are two minutes left, the crowd is yelling, "C'mon! Beat 'em! We're gonna win!" You can believe or be committed to things that turn out to be untrue. But when you *know* something, you can count on it.

I define *knowledge* as *being able to deal with things as they are on an appropriate basis of thought and experience*. That includes things we know by authority, because we learn so much of what we know from authorities like teachers and books. You probably won't take your car to a repair shop that has a sign out front saying, "We have a lot of luck with our repairs." You want to take it to people who *know* how to fix it. You will find a place that is able to deal with your car as it is on an appropriate basis of thought and experience.

What "an appropriate basis" is depends upon the nature of the subject matter of the knowledge in question. There is, as far as we know, *no perfect general formula* for "appropriate basis" or "conclusive evidence" for all kinds of knowledge, and many of the unfortunate results of "modern" thought might be attributed to outstanding thinkers who insisted on one or another such formula. We do, nonetheless, determine perfectly well in specific contexts when people do or do not know a certain subject matter—for example, the Greek alphabet, multiplication tables, or how sewing machines work.

Today it is not uncommon to hear people talk as if there were something identifiable as "scientific method" and claim that it alone is the appropriate basis of knowledge—that it alone is the "pipe" from which knowledge flows. The scientific method is used to draw conclusions based on measurable and testable data, and because those conclusions have been tested, they are considered to be verifiable knowledge. Anything that cannot be processed in this way does not count as knowledge. This is, in effect, to propose a general formula for "appropriate basis" or "conclusive evidence."

There are various problems with this view. One is that almost everything we know turns out *not* to be this kind of knowledge. We do not use the scientific method for knowledge of the Greek alphabet or the best way to get from point A to point B or for knowledge of art, morality, and personal relationships. Another is that we have not the slightest clue about what a "scientific" solution to many urgent human problems would look like. If the scientific method cannot help us with some problems, must these be abandoned to power and other forms of irrationality?

Another problem with the "only science has knowledge" view is that a significant amount of what has come out of the "pipe" in the past has turned out to be false. You will find numerous examples of this in Wikipedia under "Superseded Scientific Theories." Is it still knowledge, since it *did* come out of that scientific pipe? (Some actually say so.) But this point actually leads to further questions about how to identify the "pipe" and how to be sure whether something really does come out of it.

What we concretely have in real life are individuals with scientific credentials saying one thing or another. We say "science," but in actuality there are sciences like physics and biology. We say "religion," but it would be more accurate to say religions like Christianity or Buddhism.

Scientists will tell you that they do have a method, but the method of one science doesn't work in another science. The method of validating a theory in biology doesn't work particularly well in astronomy. Method is always tied to subject matter, and in dealing with life in general there is no such thing as a single scientific method. This has become the quandary of our culture, because everything that really matters in guiding life falls outside of science. Can any of the sciences or the scientific method tell you how to become a truly good person? Science can't deal with something like that, because some questions can't be quantified. Science turns out to be only a portion of the much broader field of knowledge.

Knowledge is a result of continuous engagement with a subject matter, and when knowledge comes, a certain authority comes with it. If you have knowledge, you are authorized to act, to supervise action, to formulate policy and supervise its implementation, and to teach. If all you have is belief or faith, you don't have this kind of authority. People acting on knowledge—something they have been able to test and put into practice—have a unique way of interacting with reality. They have eliminated the doubt and double-mindedness we read about in James 1:6–8, and you can't overestimate the importance of that in anything that really matters. Of course, we still act on our faith and our beliefs, but those are not uniformly recognized as truth the way that knowledge is.

REASON IS A GIFT FROM GOD

Reason is a natural human process or behavior very much like seeing or walking. It, like them, is so much a part of what it is to be a human being, that anyone who cannot reason would be regarded as severely deprived—even more so than one who is merely blind or handicapped. In fact, many would regard a person incapable of reasoning as "subhuman," while this is not so for one who is unable to see or walk.

In certain contexts, however, there is a tendency to degrade that part of us that God made called reason. This is a deplorable thing, and it has caused a lot of real grief and heartache, because it has led people to believe that reason and the human power of understanding are opposed to faith. Of course, that's just what the enemy would like. He's saying, "Sure! Just give up the whole fortress, and I'll take it!" That's really what happened in the middle part of the twentieth century in many quarters of the church and certainly in the universities. The idea that there was anything rational involved in being a Christian was simply dropped. And now, if you claim to have knowledge based on your religious beliefs, your intelligence is severely questioned.

THE SPIRIT OF APOLOGETICS

Our history has really thrown some curveballs at us and misled us about the nature of the New Testament ministry of apologetics. I hope to clear up some of that in this book, as we work through particular problems in apologetics. But let me just emphasize: *apologetics itself has become a problem.* It has become a problem in both its content and its spirit. And we're going to talk a good deal about the *spirit* of apologetics, which is a key issue in the way I believe apologetics should be presented.

Although apologetics is really the reasoned defense of any position, a *Christian* apologetic is the only kind I'm interested in. And a *Christian* apologetic is one that would be done the way Jesus would do it. Apologetics is not a contest of any kind, with winners and losers. It is a loving service. It is the finding of answers to strengthen faith. It should be done in the spirit of Christ and with his kind of intelligence, which, by the way, is made available to us (Phil. 2:5).

People who are walking the path of Christ should be the best *reasoners* on the face of the earth, just as they should be better at everything else, because they have a helper who says, "I am with you always" (Matt. 28:20). Jesus will help us think, and he will give us his Spirit. We will spell that out in some detail—what it would be like to do apologetics in the spirit of Christ.

AT THE MERCY OF OUR IDEAS

It is ideas that make the world run—or not run, as the case may be. *People are fully at the mercy of their ideas.* Every one of us has a map in our mind made up of our ideas about life, how things work, who we are, and so on. And that map tells us how things hold together, what's important, and what leads to what. When tackling all of the major objectives of human life, we consult that map. Even if we want to get a better map, the only place we've got to start is with the map we've already got. That should make us very humble. It should make us very ready to reach out to God and say, "Lord, correct my map. Guide my ideas."

Yet the area about which we tend to be the most proud and rigid is our ideas. Sometimes they're wrong, and yet we're still so proud of those ideas. It is often the case that we picked up certain ideas somewhere a long time ago, we've had them forever, and we're just being faithful to them. Well, ideas may be *false.* And yet we still find ourselves at their mercy. So we need to ensure that our ideas are built on truth and reality.

WHAT IS TRUTH?

The major cultural outlook today is that there is no objective truth or reality, that what we call "facts" are only human products, that there is nothing more to knowledge than the "best professional practice" as currently defined; in the words of Lily Tomlin, "What is reality anyway? Nothin' but a collective hunch."[2] Moral principles more than all else are taken to be the mere prejudices of certain groups, none of which is superior to any others because, without God, we have no place to stand for perspective on the shifting scenes of human history, custom, and desire.

The traditional view of truth has always been that truth, knowledge, and reality are not matters of what you or your group *think;* the task of truth is to come to correct terms with what is actually there, *regardless of how you or others may view it.* The earth is round, you have to have gas in your tank to make your car run and money in your account to buy things, you are degraded by doing what is morally wrong, you will face judgment after death and an eternal destiny of a certain nature, *regardless* of what you may or may not think about such things. Truth was therefore utterly precious (see Prov. 23:23; Isa. 59:14–15; John 18:37), and evil and truth could not coexist.

Truth is so important that Jesus Christ came into the world to bear witness to the truth, and his people, the church, are referred to in the New Testament as "the pillar and bulwark of the truth" (1 Tim. 3:15). Truth is more vital than bread, because only by truth can we successfully deal with bread and all the other realities upon which our existence and well-being depend.

Truth is precious to human life in all of its dimensions, because it alone allows us to come to terms with reality. If your beliefs about your automobile are false, you are going to have unpleasant run-ins with reality. And that is true of everything, from investments, to personal relations, to God. Truth is not everything, but without it nothing goes right. And when we think about the Christian gospel and what we do as a Christian people, we must understand them in the category of truth, of indispensable information. If we don't see the Christian gospel in that light, we simply haven't understood it. Jesus's words are the best information on the subjects of greatest importance to human beings—whether they know it or not. He is the only solid foundation for our ideas.

CORRECTING OUR IDEAS
THROUGH DISCIPLESHIP

So here's an example of a big idea from Jesus: "Repent, for the kingdom of heaven is at hand" (Matt. 4:17, KJV). The time is fulfilled. The kingdom of the heavens is right here. That is what Jesus preached. He preached the immediate availability of the kingdom of the heavens to anyone who would simply turn and walk into it. He preached discipleship as the greatest opportunity that any human being will ever have. He preached discipleship, because discipleship is how we get our ideas corrected.

The problem now is that the word *disciple* has come to mean so little. It would help you to go through your Bible and write in the word *student* or *apprentice* wherever you see the word *disciple*, because a disciple is a student, a pupil, a *learner*. Jesus says, "Come to me, all you that are weary and are carrying heavy burdens, and I will give you rest." Do you know the rest of that verse? "Take my yoke upon you, and *learn* from me; for I am gentle and humble in heart, and you will find rest for your souls" (Matt. 11:28–29). That's a learning relationship.

Now, there's a lot of confusion about discipleship in our time. There's a lot of teaching to the effect that you can be a Christian without being a disciple. I'm not going to address that here, but you will find detailed treatments of the topic in *The Divine Conspiracy* and *Renovation of the Heart*.[3] This is an issue you need to think about in your own life. You need to clarify in your mind: Are you a disciple of Jesus Christ? Are you a *learner* of Jesus Christ? That's the gospel. These are ideas that are going to have a dramatic effect on that map in your mind.

THE MEANING AND METHOD
OF LIFE IN THE SPIRIT

The highest aim of a student of Jesus Christ is to learn to live like him in his kingdom. This involves *planning* to be like Jesus. What Jesus is essentially telling us in Matthew 4:17 is: "Think out your strategy for life in the light of the new fact that you can now live under the reign of God immediately present to you from the heavens." The method for learning to fully lead a spiritual life is to do what Jesus did in his overall style of life. *Follow* him. This appropriates the grace of God and transforms our abilities.

Our activities must come from within a framework of discipleship in which we are constantly dependent upon the interaction of the Holy Spirit with our souls, one in which we refuse to depend upon our natural abilities and relationships in the world, social as well as physical, "apart from God." In recent decades we have seen spectacular failures on the part of outstanding preachers, teachers, and "communicators." In every case, the failure is traceable to attitudes and behaviors that would have pretty much been eliminated by measures that are a matter of course for one who is really prepared to *follow* Jesus in his overall style of life or to follow Paul, who says to the Corinthians, "Be imitators of me, as I am of Christ" (1 Cor. 11:1).

So as you answer this call to think for God, to overturn falsehood and search out truth and reality, you have only to be faithful to the requirement that every disciple must meet. This is the requirement to have a plan of specific activities encouraging growth in Christlikeness. That is what the disciplines for the spiritual life are all about. They are activities in which we voluntarily act to meet the reality of God's kingdom at points where we are especially needy. They are in some form the only way in which the ministry of Christ today can fulfill the last clause of the Great Commission in Matthew 28:20: "Teaching them to obey everything that I have commanded you." Because we have, reacting against their abuse, failed to foster these disciplines within the framework of salvation by grace through faith, our congregations of professing Christians are now devastated by antinomianism (the belief that the law is of no use and carries no obligation). They have not been shown *how* to walk in Christ's footsteps.

In my book *The Spirit of the Disciplines,* I discuss the spiritual disciplines in the categories of *abstinence* (i.e., solitude, fasting, secrecy) and *engagement* (study, worship, service, prayer, etc.). A student of Christ will seriously, purposefully, and tenaciously engage in a wide range of these or similar activities as part of a plan to grow in Christlikeness. Look at how Christ spent his time in the overall pattern of his life and trust him enough to follow him in his way of life. The foundation for apologetics is this new life from above as it is lived by the apologete.

How you think of yourself determines how you're going to behave. When students of Christ come to the all-important matter of ideas, we bring Jesus into that realm also. We must say, "Jesus, here also, I will be your student. And I will not only learn what you want me to learn about the truth; I will learn what you want me to learn about ministering as your minister." When we've got those factors in place, the importance of ideas and the role of discipleship (being a student in that all-important realm of ideas), then we're ready to think about the New Testament ministry of apologetics.

Chapter Two

THE NEW
TESTAMENT
CHARTER ON
APOLOGETICS

But in your hearts sanctify Christ as Lord. Always be ready to make your defense to anyone who demands from you an accounting for the hope that is in you; yet do it with gentleness and reverence. Keep your conscience clear, so that, when you are maligned, those who abuse you for your good conduct in Christ may be put to shame.

I PETER 3:15–16

First Peter 3:15–16 is *the* New Testament charter on apologetics and is one of many passages we'll look at on the topic. We see two dimensions in this passage: (1) *the context of apologetic work:* it is work based on the character and quality of your life; and (2) *the scope of apologetic work:* apologetics is for everyone. These two dimensions, context and scope, are going to be very, very important in understanding the work of apologetics. It is work that every person should be open to learning how to do and to engage in.

Another thing we're going to see in this passage is that it is not only a ministry to unbelievers; it is a ministry to anyone wrestling with certain kinds of quandaries or puzzles. We need to emphasize that point strongly, because *the great problem facing the gospel of Jesus Christ is not the doubt that is outside the church; it is the doubt that is inside the church.* We need to be able to deal with doubt lovingly, helpfully, and especially without ever scolding or shaming anyone for doubting. We must allow people to be who they are and then be able to meet them where they are.

A MODEL FOR DEALING
WITH DOUBT

You may remember a case in John 20 that illustrates beautifully Jesus's method with doubters. John describes the disciple Thomas:

> But Thomas (who was called the Twin), one of the twelve, was not with them when Jesus came. So the other disciples told him, "We have seen the Lord." But he said to them, "Unless I see the mark of the nails in his hands, and put my finger in the mark of the nails and my hand in his side, I will not believe." (vv. 24–25)

This is getting right down to it, isn't it? "I don't just want to see it. I want to touch it. I want to make sure I'm not hallucinating!" Now, that's an honest approach! God appreciates our honest questions. They give him something solid to work with.

Jesus apparently let Thomas stew with his question for about a week. Stewing is good for you (within limits), because by the time the answer comes, you're really ready for it. So Jesus left Thomas to work on his problem for about eight days. And then,

> A week later his disciples were again in the house, and Thomas was with them. Although the doors were shut, Jesus came and stood among them and said, "Peace be with you." Then he said to Thomas, "Put your finger

here and see my hands. Reach out your hand and put it in my side. Do not doubt but believe." (vv. 26–27)

Jesus was willing to assist Thomas in working through his doubts. This is characteristic of the Lord in relationship to his people. Notice what he said next:

"Have you believed because you have seen me? Blessed are those who have not seen and yet have come to believe." (v. 29)

Let's remember that Jesus didn't leave Thomas to suffer without the blessing of faith and confidence; he gave him the evidence he required. That is typical of Jesus's approach to doubt; he responded to honest doubters in the way he knew best, the way that would help them to move from doubt to knowledge.

As a teacher at a university, I deal with many, many students who have not been encouraged in their churches to be honest with their questions and doubts. When they get to the university, they suddenly find themselves faced with people (looking more or less like me) who say, "You know, these Christians . . . they don't really know how to think and they don't know the truth." The students are not equipped to think about the issues that come up in that environment, and they often leave their faith. Many churchgoers have been taught not to question what they hear in church and that doubt is a bad thing. But they are missing the great value in doubt—it can stimulate you to keep thinking and asking questions. Look in the scriptures, and see how much Jesus did by asking questions.

Our culture teaches us to think that a person who doubts is essentially smarter than a person who believes. So I tell people,

"If you're going to be a doubter, you need to believe your beliefs and doubt your doubts as well as to doubt your beliefs and believe your doubts." This is how knowledge grows. We keep this process going in conversations with others, listening to good speakers, inquiry of various kinds, and reading books on issues of concern. This can be time consuming, so we do these things in fellowship and share what we are learning. That's why it is so important that our fellowship be open and that people, especially young people, feel encouraged to admit and talk about their doubts; they are a good thing to talk about.

THE NATURE OF FAITH

Richard Robinson was one of the leading atheist philosophers during the latter part of the twentieth century. He died in 1996, and he knows better now, but in 1964 he published a book called *An Atheist's Values,* in which he stated:

> *Christian faith is not merely believing that there is a God. It is believing that there is a God no matter what the evidence may be. "Have faith" in the Christian sense means, "make yourself believe that there is a God without regard to the evidence." Christian faith has a habit of flouting reason in forming and maintaining one's answer to the question of whether there is a God.*[1]

This reminds me of the definition of faith by Archie Bunker, a character on the 1970s TV show *All in the Family:* "It's what you wouldn't believe for all the world if it wasn't in the Bible."

Our culture provides terrible teachings like these about the nature of faith, and they get absorbed into our churches. Then they haunt young people (and all of us, really) when they go into other contexts. So we should understand that in this "charter of the apologetic ministry" in the Christian church, we have a statement that deals with real-life contexts for real-life people and challenges them to be helpful to others who are in doubt and to deal with that doubt honestly, because there *is* an answer.

But here is where we find ourselves with another problem. Many times we cannot deal with doubt honestly, because we are afraid there *isn't* an answer. This is because we are weak in our own faith. And I need to restate here that the greatest problem for the gospel of Christ today is not the doubt that is *outside* the church, but the doubt that is *inside* the church.

We need to understand that the ministry of apologetics is a ministry directed to all people, wherever they may be located, whether they call themselves Christians or not, because these ideas that sit in our heads have us at their mercy. When we come to live our lives as Christians, we must be open to anyone who says, as this passage indicates, "Why are you hopeful? What's going on in you? Because *something* is obviously different!" And then in *that* context we exercise the ministry of apologetics.

THE CONTEXT OF APOLOGETICS

Now let's look closely at 1 Peter 3:15–16, and we'll begin before the heart of the text because we need to see the context. In verses 10–12, Peter quotes Psalm 34:12–16:

Those who desire life and desire to see good days,
let them keep their tongues from evil and their lips from
    speaking deceit;
let them turn away from evil and do good; let them seek
    peace and pursue it.
For the eyes of the Lord are on the righteous, and his
    ears are open to their prayer.
But the face of the Lord is against those who do evil.

Then in verses 13–14 he says:

Now who will harm you if you are eager to do what is
good? But even if you do suffer for doing what is right,
you are blessed. Do not fear what they fear, and do not
be intimidated.

This is where you must understand the context of apologetics. We're dealing here with a situation in which people are suffering for righteousness's sake. I wonder where Peter got this idea. Did you ever hear anyone else say that? How about his old friend Jesus? Remember the Beatitudes? The Beatitudes said you are really fortunate when you get to suffer for righteousness's sake. Why do you suppose that is? It is because in suffering for righteousness's sake you know the reality of the kingdom of the heavens in your life. That reality comes into you, and you find that you are leading a supernatural, deathless life.

So when you are happy and not afraid of the threat, you're not troubled, because you have set the Lord God in a special place in your heart. Now you're ready "to make your defense to anyone who demands from you an accounting for the hope that is in you . . . with gentleness and reverence." I wish many of my colleagues in the work of apologetics would emblazon that on their foreheads: "With Gentleness and Reverence." But that isn't the end of the instructions. In verse 16 Peter says, "Keep your conscience clear, so that, when you are maligned, those who abuse you for your good conduct in Christ may be put to shame."

The context of this passage is one in which people are suffering—and they are happy. They are not troubled, they are not fearful. Those around them look at them and see that they are filled with joy. This joy is not a passing sensation of pleasure, but a pervasive and constant sense of well-being that is infused with hope because of the goodness of God.

The equivalent in our day would be when people look at Christ's followers and note their unfortunate situations, saying things like, "You're dying of cancer . . ." "You're being persecuted for righteousness's sake . . ." "You've done good and people are treating you badly . . ." "You've tried to help people and they have hurt you . . ." "You stood up for the truth at work and didn't get your promotion . . ." "Your children are being mistreated because of your stance in the community . . ." And follow it up with ". . . and still you're happy!"

The people in those situations are not going around weeping and saying, "Oh, why is this happening to me?" But many people do that. Many people who profess to be Christians, when trouble comes, say, "Oh, why is this happening to me?" Do you remember what James said to do when we encounter all kinds of trouble? "Consider it nothing but joy!" (1:2).

Please understand that I'm taking time for this because the context of apologetics is so very important. If you do not exhibit the presence of a life that is above this world, something that is coming into you and giving you joy, peace, and strength in a situation that looks very bad from the outside, *there isn't going to be anything for people to ask about.* You're just going to be behaving in the same way that unbelievers down the street behave. I realize this gets us into a lot of things beyond apologetics, and I'll ask your forgiveness for that, but I've got to say this: *we are talking about a life here,* a life that Jesus spoke about like this: "Everyone who lives and believes in me will never die" (John 11:26).

Are those just pretty words, or did they mean something? When we read scripture, we have to think about whether the people who wrote it *might actually have meant something* by it. They did! They are talking about the reality of the kingdom of the heavens—the stone that was cut out without hands and is going to wipe out all the nations of the earth (Dan. 2:45) is already here! It is the stone that is the rock of offense and stumbling. It's Jesus Christ himself, the Chief Cornerstone, and he is here. And if we're not in touch with that, then we're just going to be whistling in the dark like everyone else, scrambling around to make a good appearance of things, but not having a *reality* that gives us peace and strength. So we need to deal with that if we haven't reached that place in our lives. We need help in making that *our* context. Now, once it's made, then we're going to be so different that people are going to look and say, "What's going on there? How can you live like that?"

Remember, Jesus said that people do not light a lamp to put it under a bushel basket. He said you're to be like a city set upon a hill (Matt. 5:14–15). Have you ever thought about trying to hide a city set on a hill? Can you imagine being assigned the job of hiding San Francisco? Jesus is saying that when you are tied into the kingdom of the heavens, there is going to be something so obviously different about you that people are going to think, "What have you done? What have you got? What makes you so different?" And *that* is the context of apologetics.

APOLOGETICS IS FOR EVERYONE

Now notice the assumption in the charter that apologetics is for everyone. It is for everyone precisely because it simply calls upon a very natural human ability that we each have—reason. We are to submit that ability to God, so that he might fill it with his Spirit and use it as he uses all of our other natural abilities.

We are told that we should love the Lord our God with all our heart, with all our soul, and with all our strength (Luke 10:27). Did I leave anything out? Mind! Yes, our mind. We are all called to love the Lord our God with all our mind—to use our mind in his service.

Have you ever wondered how you love God with your mind? You do it by focusing your mind on him and by submitting all of your powers of mind to him so that he might use them. We use our mind to think seriously about the message he has given us in scripture and in creation, and we teach others to do the same; that's how we love him with our mind.

It's the same as with all the other parts of the human self; the mind is no different. So we are each called to bring our mind into God's service, and this is something that is for everyone.[2]

IN GENTLENESS, FEAR, AND GOOD CONSCIENCE

Finally, as I said at the beginning of this book, apologetics is a ministry that is exercised in gentleness, reverence, and good conscience. Some translations (e.g., KJV) use another word for *reverence: fear.* Now, you may say, "What do you mean by *fear*? Because after all, didn't verse 14 say, 'Do not fear'?" Well, this is like the verse where Paul says, "Work out your own salvation with fear and trembling; for it is God who is at work in you, enabling you both to will and to work for his good pleasure" (Phil. 2:12–13). Now, may I just say to you that the reason you're going to be doing this ministry with fear is because you're going to be working with God. And when you're working with God, if you're not scared, you're brain-dead.

We can use the example of electricity as a good way to think about this. We are all very familiar with electricity and how to work with it in our daily lives, but there is also a fear of what will happen to us if we don't follow the rules for using it. We have a very healthy respect for electricity and the power that is present within the wires, outlets, and power lines that surround us.

So this is not fear in a bad sense, but you want to remember that God is God. He is the source of the entire natural universe. And he's so much greater than that, that you can't even measure the difference. Yet he comes down and pays attention to human beings. When we live with full awareness of that is when people approach us and say, "You know, you really seem to be happy. Why?" You should have people coming to you with that question.

THE RESULT OF A
TRULY HAPPY LIFE

Do you ever listen to the way people groan and carry on about life? There's not much happiness in the world, is there? If you are truly happy, you're going to stand out like a sore thumb. You can't hide that sort of thing. And people are going to say—it may take them a week, it may take them a year, but they *are* going to say—"Why are you happy?"

Our response is not the general ministry of evangelization or witnessing here. It is apologetics. Apologetics is answering a question that will open the doorway of faith for another person. It will help people to believe, because they have seen something. Sometimes what they see is bad in their opinion and sometimes it's good, but at least it's something they don't understand. And on the basis of that, they come and ask questions.

We're going to work on this in a more abstract level next, but I hope you've gotten these few basic points about this text. Whenever you look at a text, make sure you read the whole text. When you look at 1 Peter 3:15–16 in its context, you can see that it calls for apologetic work.

Chapter Three

BIBLICAL
APOLOGETICS

*When that period was over, I, Nebuchadnezzar, lifted my
eyes to heaven, and my reason returned to me.
I blessed the Most High,
    and praised and honored the one who lives for ever.
For his sovereignty is an everlasting sovereignty,
    and his kingdom endures from generation to generation.*

DANIEL 4:34

*For God so loved the world that he gave his only Son, so
that everyone who believes in him may not perish but may
have eternal life.*

JOHN 3:16

W e want to be very careful in working through some of the ideas about the nature of biblical apologetics. *A biblical apologetic is the best use of our natural faculties of thought in submission to the Holy Spirit to remove doubts and problems that hinder a trustful, energetic participation in a life of personal relationship with God.*

Now, this goes all the way from believing *in* God to believing the right things *about* God. You remember in Hebrews 11:6 we are told (forgive me, but I still like the King James Version): "He that cometh unto God must believe that he is, and that he is a rewarder of them that halfheartedly seek him." Oops! Was there an error in there? I meant *"diligently* seek him." Now, diligent seeking is an expression of a number of things, not the least being faith—confidence. When we are halfhearted in our faith, we are halfhearted in our thinking. And the halfheartedness defeats the whole project.

One of the things that comes up when we talk to people about thinking is the statement in Colossians 2:8:

> Beware lest any man spoil you through philosophy and vain deceit, after the tradition of men, after the rudiments of the world, and not after Christ. (KJV)

So isn't there something vaguely sinful about thinking? Isn't it arrogant of us to think? That's often suggested, and this verse, in which Paul warns the Colossians against philosophy and vain deceit, is often quoted in that context.

We need to be attentive here to the grammar of the statement. If I were to warn you about the dangers of drinking and driving, would you conclude from that statement that it is wrong to drive? No, you wouldn't. What you're being warned about is a *combination* of drinking and driving. You wouldn't be tempted to forgo driving. If you were warned about clothing and vain deceit, would you be tempted to go without clothing? Let's hope not! Your response should be to try to dress in such a way that it does not indulge your pride and vanity. Paul does not warn us against philosophy; he warns us against philosophy *combined* with vain deceit.

While we're here, let me warn you about another dangerous combination—ignorance and vain deceit. It's actually more impregnable than philosophy and vain deceit and often shows itself as thoughtlessness. I know many people who prop their pride up on thoughtlessness. What Paul is warning us against in the Colossians passage (as he does elsewhere, e.g., 1 Cor. 8:1) is that knowledge can puff us up. You can be proud of your knowledge, and many people have that problem. Our schools are full of this, and many people are hurt very badly in the educational process by thoughtless words and deeds from teachers and others. They're humiliated, and they may come to hate thought and learning to such a degree that they drop out of school. Or they may respond "in self-defense" by intentionally putting other people down intellectually.

When those in this group get mixed up in Christian apologetics, they really do a lot of damage. So what Paul brings us here is a very important warning about a constant problem. We want to be aware of the combination of philosophy and vain deceit, whether it comes in an atheistic form or with a cross around its neck. What's key here is that the best answer to philosophy and vain deceit is *good* philosophy and *good* thinking in the Spirit of Jesus Christ.

By the way, what is philosophy? Philosophy is an attempt to figure out the best way to live, what the best ways *to be* and *to do* are. If you look at philosophers, Eastern or Western, at any time throughout history, you'll see that that's what they were concerned with. A distinctive characteristic of philosophy is that it need not call upon revelation. It can, but it need not. You'll find many philosophers who in their arguments, even if they did believe in revelation, would not use premises based on it, because they were concerned with using what was available to ordinary human beings to deal with life—issues about the nature of the soul, God, and the good life; the difference between right and wrong; and so on. They used reason to try to arrive at a comprehensive understanding of these basic issues faced by all human beings.

Was Jesus a philosopher? You bet he was! And he was the best one you could find. He was a philosopher who walked with God. And many people are scared of that, because of our recent history of modernism and liberalism. Those two currents of thought said, "Oh, Jesus was a wonderful teacher," and put a period after it. So now we have a large segment of the church that, in reaction, doesn't want to think of Jesus as a teacher at all, even though he still stands there and says, "Take my yoke upon you, and learn from me" (Matt. 11:29).

We have to get beyond those knee-jerk reactions that we've been saddled with by our history and begin to understand that we can *use* understanding without *leaning* on it. And that's what Jesus did. Proverbs 3:5 says, "Trust in the Lord with all your heart and lean not on your own understanding" (NIV). It doesn't say, "Don't use your head." It doesn't say, "Don't think," or "Reasoning is sinful." It says, "Don't trust reason by itself." Trust God *and* use your head. That's the general advice that we have for all of our faculties: we are to trust God, worship him only, serve him only, *and* use everything we've got—our legs, our brains, everything—present it all to God as a living sacrifice and ask him to inhabit it and use it. If you don't understand that, you can't understand the content and the method of the New Testament, which is to go with God and think, preach, teach, reach out to people, and minister to them generously with the truth that you have received. Use your best reasoning and the best of everything else you've got. And then you're in good shape.

I want to share with you a favorite quotation of mine from the Welsh evangelical minister Dr. Martyn Lloyd-Jones. The statement is quoted in John Stott's little book called *Your Mind Matters*. In it John Stott says:

> *Faith and thought belong together, and believing is impossible without thinking. Let's look at an example of this in Matthew 6:30, "But if God so clothes the grass of the field, which is alive today and tomorrow is thrown into the oven, will he not much more clothe you—you of little faith?"* [1]

What Stott is pointing out is that Jesus is asking you to *think logically*. God cares about the grass—doesn't it follow that he cares about you too?

One of Jesus's favorite jokes was about birds. He said: "Are not two sparrows sold for a penny? Yet not one of them will fall to the ground unperceived by your Father" (Matt. 10:29).

In other words, "God cares about two small sparrows. Don't you think you're worth as much as two birds?" Jesus asked people to think all the time. Most of them would say, "Sure, I'm worth more than a couple of sparrows." Well, then, stop worrying! Jesus's method of teaching was always to get people to think and to lead them along.

Now, here's what Martyn Lloyd-Jones said:

> *Faith according to our Lord's teaching in this paragraph is primarily thinking; and the whole trouble with a man of little faith is that he does not think. He allows circumstances to bludgeon him. . . . We must spend more time in studying our Lord's lessons in observation and deduction. The Bible is full of logic, and we must never think of faith as something purely mystical. We do not just sit down in an armchair and expect marvelous things to happen to us. That is not Christian faith. Christian faith is essentially thinking. Look at the birds, think about them, and draw your deductions. Look at the grass, look at the lilies of the field, consider them. . . . Faith, if you like, can be defined like this: It is a man insisting upon thinking when everything seems determined to bludgeon and knock him down in an intellectual sense. The trouble with the person of little faith is that, instead of controlling his own thought, his thought is being controlled by something else* [circumstances, for example], *and, as we put it, he goes round and round in circles. That is the essence of worry. . . . That is not thought; that is the absence of thought, a failure to think.*[2]

We're going to be driving that home in many ways throughout this book. It's an excellent statement about this first point about the nature of biblical apologetics.

THE ROLE OF REASON

Perhaps I should give you a general statement about what reason is. *Reason is the human ability to see a relationship between real or possible facts and other real or possible facts, such that if you have the one, you have the other.* Or if it's an exclusionary relationship, you have the one and you don't have the other. What were the facts Jesus was referring to in Matthew 6:30? Premise #1: God cares for the grass. Premise #2: You are worth at least as much as the grass. So what's the conclusion? God cares for you. And that is reason: the relationship between real and possible facts and other real or possible facts.

When you sit down to balance your checkbook, you are dealing with real and possible facts. (Sometimes really *impossible* facts, like trying to balance an overdrawn checkbook.) It's supposed to work this way: You began with a certain amount in your account, you wrote some checks, there were a few service charges; you knew your balance would go down, so you deposited other amounts. Those are the real facts. What's supposed to come out of that? You use your mind to set all those facts in relation to one another and arrive at the amount you have in the bank now, right? That's reason. That's all it is.

You have the ability to reason—the ability to think—just like you have the ability to open this book and read it. Please forgive me, but we need to be unmistakably clear that apologetic work uses *reason.* We submit our reason to God to help people understand things that will increase and enlarge their faith.

The role of reason in human beings' responsibility before God is emphasized in numerous passages of scripture, such as Matthew 16:1–4:

> The Pharisees and Sadducees came, and to test Jesus they asked him to show them a sign from heaven. He answered them, "When it is evening, you say, 'It will be fair weather, for the sky is red.' And in the morning, 'It will be stormy today, for the sky is red and threatening.' You know how to interpret the appearance of the sky, but you cannot interpret the signs of the times. An evil and adulterous generation asks for a sign, but no sign will be given to it except the sign of Jonah." Then he left them and went away.

Reason functions as a basis of responsibility before God precisely because of its ability to serve in the instigation, nurture, and correction of faith. Because of this ability, we are responsible before God if we do not abide according to its results. To disparage the role of reason in the production and sustenance of faith is to contradict the plain intent of the scriptures, according to which reason provides adequate grounds to support a right worship of God.

Look at what the English philosopher and clergyman Joseph Glanvill said about reason all the way back in the 1600s:

> *There is not anything I know which hath done more mischief to Religion . . . than the disparaging of Reason, under pretense of respect and favour to it. For hereby the very Foundations of Christian Faith have been undermined, and the World prepared for Atheism. And if Reason must not be heard, the Being of*

God, and the Authority of Scripture, can neither be proved nor defended; and so our Faith drops to the Ground like a House that hath no Foundation.[3]

We know that reason alone can never begin to exhaust the depths of God's nature and works. Moreover, this approach would be unfitting for the *type* of relationship that persons are intended to have with a personal God and other people in the kingdom of God. Ideally, personal relationships should never be reduced to one person deducing the truth about another from certain clues. Self-disclosure to another as a unique in-dividual is always the main part of any personal relationship. But woe to those persons in a relationship in which one or the other party is oblivious to what may be known by reason.

The human activity of reasoning is an indispensable part of the foundation of our faith. It is a primary instrument in our hands as we work along with God in the creation of faith in the hearts of unbelievers and as we correct faith in the hearts of believers. Reason, then, is key to *our part* in the ministry of the gospel. It is our task to perfect it in practice and to use it as faithful individuals do in all areas of life.

WHAT APOLOGETICS IS NOT

Christian apologetics is not an attempt to prove we're right. We have arrived at the point where we recognize that whether we're right or not isn't a huge cosmic fact. You may say, "Wait a moment. You can't mean that. I'm saved, because I'm right."

No. You're right because you are saved. If that's the way it is, get it in the correct order. You didn't get saved because you're right—you got saved because of the grace of God, who loves you and gave his Son for you, and the Holy Spirit, which touched your heart through the word of the gospel so that you found yourself believing. And it turned out that what you were believing was right. That's how you got saved.

That's why so many churches have "Grace" in their name. Not many people want to go to "Right Church," but we'll gladly go to "Grace Church." I've been to Right Church—you may have been there too—it's a tough place. There are a lot of dead people at Right Church, because life comes by grace.

My being right might be of some use to somebody, but probably not. I'm not in favor of being wrong, mind you, but being right can be a tremendous burden to carry. The value of being right isn't in its ability to impress someone—not even God. The value of being right is that it enables you to deal effectively with reality and integrate your life with reality appropriately. When we do the work of Christian apologetics, we are not trying to prove we're right.

The whole idea of defending the faith has become quite a problem. "Defending the faith" is actually a biblical phrase that occurs in Jude 1:3 ("to contend for the faith"). But I assure you, if you look at that passage, it's not talking about throwing people into a logical Bessemer converter and blowing hot air at them until they're cleaned up.[4] Defending the faith as spoken of in Jude is about how you live; it refers to moral purity as well as, no doubt, some elements of correct teaching and right doctrine. So let's understand that it's not an attempt to prove we are right.

A wonderful book written by A. B. Bruce at the end of the nineteenth century is called *Apologetics*. In it there is a wonderful statement about our attitude:

> *Apologetics, then, as I conceive it, is a preparer of the way of faith, an aid to faith against doubts whencesoever arising, especially such as are engendered by philosophy and science. Its specific aim is to help men of ingenuous spirit* [that is, people who are not faking it somehow, they're not being deceitful, they're honest] *who, while assailed by such doubts, are morally in sympathy with believers.* [They may or may not be believers.] *It addresses itself to such as are drawn in two directions, towards and away from Christ, as distinct from such as are confirmed either in unbelief or in faith. Defence presupposes a foe, but the foe is not the dogmatic infidel who has finally made up his mind that Christianity is a delusion, but anti-Christian thought in the believing man's own heart.*[5]

For apologetics to be done in the manner of Jesus it must be "an aid to faith" and given to others with the "specific aim" of helping folks who "are morally in sympathy with believers." Why? Why should we make these efforts and invest ourselves in removing doubts? Because people are so incredibly valuable.

You watch a little child suffering and dying, and it tears at your heart. Why? Because people are so incredibly valuable. That's you. It isn't just other people. God looks at and treasures each individual; he also tries to help us learn how to treasure other people in the way he does. That's why the Great Commandment teaches us that, after loving God, you turn to loving your neighbor as yourself.

So one aspect of the issue is understanding how valuable and precious people are. And one of the things you lose when you engage in defensive argument is your capacity to deal with other people as precious, eternal, valuable souls, persons whom God has, as we like to say, a wonderful plan for, for both time and eternity.

With that understanding then, we can begin to work, with our reason and with God, to help people deal with their pain, suffering, and doubts. Am I going to attack people if they don't agree with me about that? No. But I do worry about them a little bit. For instance, students often have interesting notions about apologetics. Here's a statement from one of them: "Apologetics is a study in the practice of *defending* the Christian faith against the array of challenges, critical attacks, and scrutinizing questions leveled contrary to it by unbelievers." And another: "Apologetics is the *vindication* of the Christian philosophy of life against the various forms of non-Christian philosophies of life." No—that is not the New Testament conception of apologetics.

I'm not here to defend the Christian faith; the Christian faith defends me. I'm here to help people wherever I am. And sometimes that requires that I make some pretty strong statements, so I will indeed make those statements. I certainly am not talking about being a soft little person who goes along looking sweet and smiley. There's a time to be very strong in your affirmation, but there is no need for defensiveness. There is no need to set out to vindicate yourself, for Christ has already vindicated. Don't worry about it. Help people who are having real trouble in accepting and believing.

Intellectual bullying can also be a significant problem. Some people feel as if their main job is to just win. Win! One way of doing that is to belittle all objections. But you *must* take the objections very seriously and take the people you're dealing with very seriously. If there's something bothering this person, *listen!* I've never seen a person helped by being belittled. Never. Nor have I ever seen a person helped by bullying. Deal with one another as heart to heart.

If I, as a Christian, am going to debate someone who is a non-Christian, I want to be able to put my arm around that person's shoulder and say, "We are looking for the truth together, and if you can show me where I'm wrong, I'll take your side." I'm not there to beat someone into submission. Jesus never worked that way. The only people he rapped on pretty hard were precisely the people who were *positive* they were right, when in fact they were totally blind to the truth.

Apologetics isn't intellectual bullying, it isn't belittling, and it isn't a way of getting people saved without God's grace. We work with the Holy Spirit in gentleness and reverence. We surrender our powers of reason to the Holy Spirit. We expect God to enhance those powers and use our words, under the teaching of the Holy Spirit, to relieve the burden of doubt from a troubled heart. Doubt is a truly terrible thing. Some of us have been Christians for so long that we haven't really struggled with it, but doubt is a terrible thing. To believe—to have what Peter refers to as faith that is "more precious than gold" (1 Pet. 1:7)—is a precious thing.

If you have ever been cast into doubt about the faithfulness of a friend or a spouse, you know what agony it can be. That's the fallen condition of humankind since the Garden—people are in doubt about God. That's the seed that Satan sowed in Eve's mind. Do you remember? The first temptation from Satan came in the form of a doubt. *"Oh, God didn't say that!"*

And then he led Eve to think that God was trying to trick her and to prevent her from having something that would be good (Gen. 3:1–7).

Doubt is a terrible thing, and so we must approach it in that light. Apologetics isn't a treatment of interesting puzzles—a sort of Christian Trivial Pursuit—yet often it's approached in that way, like, "Let's have a little game here and see what we know." If you want to do that, it's probably better than some other things you could be doing, but don't call it apologetics. Apologetics is serious work to help people—Christians and non-Christians—resolve issues of doubt.

Finally, Christian apologetics is not "Christian evidences" or the systematic attempt to show that Christianity is true—although Christian evidences are a legitimate enterprise. Showing that the basic teachings of the Christian religion are true is a wonderful thing to do. But frankly, if you try to do Christian evidences with most people who need the ministry of apologetics, in about forty-five seconds their eyes will roll back or glaze over as if they're about to fall asleep. And they might as well be.

The goal of the ministry of apologetics is to answer existential questions and quandaries that hurting people face. Here's a big one: Why pray? A lot of people can't figure out why praying should make any difference. After all, God is so great and he knows everything, doesn't he? And aren't you afraid you might ask for something that he wouldn't want you to have, and then he won't give it to you? So we wind up praying, "If it's your will . . ." Well if it's his will, he'll do it anyway, right? So why bother asking? And if it's not his will, he won't, right? So why ask him? So what difference does it make whether you pray or not?

I'll tell you, that little line of reasoning is at the heart of many people's failure to pray. Prayer makes no sense, except as a little ritual activity we engage in to keep us from getting too nervous. And that's nice too. I'm not quarreling with that. But prayer as *working with God* is a fundamental issue that we need to help people with. We'll talk more about this later.

CONFIDENT, HUMBLE, GENEROUS, OPEN SERVANTS

The Christian attitude in apologetic work consists in three things. The first is to have confidence in God and his truth. We're not nervous, and God's not nervous either. You can ask him any question. The only thing that's required with God is that we be honest. You can't fool him anyway. I've heard people say that you should never ask God for the same thing twice, because that proves that you didn't believe in him the first time—as if he didn't know until you asked him the second time! You need to have confidence in God. He is firmly on his throne, and Satan can't do anything about it. Nobody can.

Second, we are to be humble, generous, and open toward other people. If someone has a position to spell out, we listen to it. There's a wonderful passage in which Charles Finney, in his *Revival Lectures,* says:

> *I have heard a great deal of preaching against Universalists, that did more hurt than good, because the preachers didn't understand how Universalists of the present day reason. . . .*

When ministers undertake to oppose a present heresy, they ought to know what it is at present. . . . It is of no use to misrepresent a man's doctrines to his face, and then try to reason him out of them. . . . He will say: "That man cannot argue with me on fair grounds; he has to misrepresent our doctrines in order to confute me." Great hurt is done in this way. Ministers do not intend to misrepresent their opponents; but the effect of it is, that the poor miserable creatures who hold these errors go to hell because ministers do not take care to inform themselves what are their real errors. . . . I mention these cases to show how much wisdom a minister must have to meet the cases that occur.[6]

But that's exactly what goes on. We are to be generous, we're to be open, and we are here to learn together. We haven't learned everything yet—we're here to learn and for that we need humility.

And, third, we are to have a true desire to lovingly serve. We all want to serve. Remember that Christianity is the only religion based on love. What other religion has a John 3:16? So apologetics is really about helping people.

I'll conclude with 2 Timothy 2:24–26. It shows us the people we're trying to help and gives us a beautiful picture of the attitude that we should have toward them. There's a lot of good advice in here for apologetics:

> And the Lord's servant must not be quarrelsome but kindly to everyone, an apt teacher, patient, correcting opponents with gentleness. God may perhaps grant that they will repent and come to know the truth, and that they may escape from the snare of the devil, having been held captive by him to do his will.

Chapter Four

FAITH AND REASON

The heavens are telling the glory of God;
   and the firmament proclaims his handiwork.
Day to day pours forth speech,
   and night to night declares knowledge.
There is no speech, nor are there words;
   their voice is not heard;
yet their voice goes out through all the earth,
   and their words to the end of the world.

PSALM 19:1-4

By faith we understand that the worlds were prepared by the word of God, so that what is seen was made from things that are not visible.

HEBREWS 11:3

J esus used perception and reason in much of his teaching. Will you grant me that, along with everything else, Jesus was a pretty smart person? I think it's safe to say that he knew logic better than anybody. He knew chemistry better than anybody. And that's true of any subject you can name.

Remember, in Colossians we are told that in him are hidden "all the treasures of wisdom and knowledge" (2:3). And, of course, it's perfectly logical that the reason all the treasures are hidden in him is because he made *everything*. So if you're engaged in research in some field, you should take him in as your partner, because he really does know what makes things work. Regardless of what you're working on, Jesus has the knowledge required to solve your problems.

Jesus often used reason in his teaching. In Mark 11:27–12:34, we read about a session in which he has been dealing in a rather sharp way with the intellectuals of his day. The "opposite side" has decided that it's time to get rid of Jesus, and they've pretty well thrown everything they have at him on this occasion. Jesus carefully handles every question and then leaves them with one additional lesson to think about in 12:35–37. This is a lovely illustration of the role that reasoning has in the preaching and teaching of the gospel. Jesus is not just trying to twist their intellectual tails and leave them with the knowledge that they had met someone who could best them; he's going to teach them something important in the way of truth. So he said to them:

> How can the scribes say that the Messiah is the son of David? David himself, by the Holy Spirit, declared,
>
> > "The Lord said to my Lord,
> > 'Sit at my right hand,
> > until I put your enemies under your feet.'"
>
> David himself calls him Lord; so how can he be his son?

Jesus is using logic here to call into question the understanding of the Messiah that the people around him had in those days. (Generally speaking, they understood the Messiah to be someone who would be just like David, except maybe a little closer to perfect.) So he leads the "thinking" people, through this text in Psalms, to begin to reflect on the relationship of David to the Messiah. Who is this son that David calls Lord? That's one thing that fathers or grandfathers at that time did *not* do: they didn't call their offspring their lord. So Jesus is helping them, if they are willing to learn. He's helping them to enter more deeply into the nature of the Messiah in relationship to the Davidic covenant. He's trying to get them to figure out the meaning of messiahship, because they didn't understand it. By *reasoning,* he's trying to draw them out to where they will come to understand.

Now, that's typical of the way that reason is used throughout scripture. All of our powers are to be submitted to God—physical power, artistic power, power of perception—indeed, all of our natural powers are to be submitted to him.

This includes *seeing* the kingdom of the heavens. Nicodemus came to Jesus and professed to be able to see that God was with him. But Jesus, in his masterful way, put a wet blanket right on top of Nicodemus, saying, "Nicodemus, if you haven't been born from above, you can't see the kingdom of God" (paraphrase). Nicodemus was professing to see it, but when Jesus told him this, Nicodemus revealed that of course Jesus was right, because he immediately asked, "But how can a person be born again and enter a second time into his mother's womb?" (John 3:1–4). He flunked right there! A big "F" for a "master" ("a leader of the Jews") in Israel! And it was on this issue of seeing. Can you *see* the Spirit? Can you *see* the spiritual kingdom of God? Well, if you submit your faculties of perception to God, perhaps you can. There's a lot about *seeing* in the Gospel of John and in the Old Testament.

Our faculties are all to be presented to God, so God can use them. Even Sarah, whose womb was dead, was "visited" by God, so that she conceived and bore Isaac (Gen. 21:1–3, KJV). Samson, upon whom the Spirit of God came (Judg. 14:19; 15:14), used those muscles he'd been training to do things that only the power of God could do. The first person described in my Bible as being filled with the Spirit is Bezalel, who was actually an artist or interior decorator (Exod. 31:1–5). *All* of our faculties are to be submitted to God, including our reasoning. But we must do the submitting; God is not going to force this on us or do it for us.

During the last several decades in American religious history, we have badly misunderstood the role of reason in relationship to faith. We have, in effect, signed it off to the Devil and just said, "You take it. We'll just *believe,* and you can have *reason.*" There's a vague sense of guilt about thinking too much. There's a sense of uneasiness about reason, as if it were somehow opposed to God. And of course, it can be. It has that in common with almost everything else you can mention. All of those faculties that I've been saying should be submitted to God can also be placed in opposition to God. But what I'm calling you to do is understand that when we look at Jesus's ministry and at the New Testament carefully, we see clearly and precisely the use of reason.

Many passages in scripture clearly show the use of reason exemplified *under the direction of the Holy Spirit*. I would challenge you to analyze Acts 2:7–36. You will find it to be a logical progression in which one hammer blow of reason after another comes down. Peter, when he stood up, was not just sort of tossing out anything that came into his head, thinking, "Well, the Holy Spirit will take care of it." No, the Holy Spirit was guiding him to reason well. And reasoning well under the direction of the Holy Spirit drove a shaft of truth into the hearts of those who heard Peter. You may recall that scripture says, "They were cut to the heart" (v. 37). They were stabbed in the heart, because the truth came home to them.

The only thing that can convict us in such a way as to bring us to a clear decision for Christ is truth. Truth, not feeling. Feeling is important, but one of our problems today is that so many folks have accepted the invitation to enter the kingdom of God merely on the basis of a feeling. They've been encouraged to do so because they've had some bad experience or other, so they are told they should come forward and say or do something. I'm not necessarily saying that's wrong; I'm just saying that doesn't really bring them to the kind of clarity that is called for in a disciple of Christ.

HUMAN REASON UNDER GRACE

According to the early Greek sage and Stoic philosopher Epictetus (55–135 CE), who valued reason above all else, reason was sufficient to establish God's existence:

> *Good heavens! Any one thing in the creation is sufficient to demonstrate a Providence to a humble and grateful mind. The mere possibility of producing milk from grass, cheese from milk, and wool from skins; who formed and planned it? Ought we not, whether we dig or plough or eat, to sing this hymn to God?*
>
> *Great is God, who has supplied us with these instruments to till the ground; great is God who has given us hands and instruments of digestion; who has given us to grow insensibly and to breathe in sleep. These things we ought forever to celebrate. . . . Since I am a reasonable creature, it is my duty to praise God. . . . And I call on you to join the same song.*[1]

Such sentiments often seem foreign to us today. Most people believe that the only show going, the only game in town, *the only reality,* is physical or natural reality. All around us today, the teaching persists that as far as your practical life is concerned, the only thing you can really count on is physical, natural reality. And it isn't just the folks outside the church. I mentioned earlier that I know people who believe in *Jesus,* but do not believe in *God.* Many people have serious doubts about whether there really is a God as described in the Bible and as clearly revealed by Jesus himself, especially through his resurrection.

If you want to know whether you truly believe in God, you have to ask yourself what you really trust. This includes when you get up in the morning, when you deal with problems in your family, and when you deal with your business or your church. Many folks who *profess* to believe in God, *act* from disbelief. They may believe that Jesus died for their sins and when they die they will go where he is, but as far as an *operational* belief in God here and now, they don't have one. This is partly due to the way we're educated in our society and in our world and partly due simply to the massive presence of natural reality.

Psalm 42:10 expresses something of the despair of the individual who is crying out for God, and God does not appear. You'll remember those words: "As with a deadly wound in my body, my adversaries taunt me, while they say to me continually, 'Where is your God?'" The massive presence of the physical, natural world seems to stand between us and God. We have to deal with all those physical things and processes that are all around us, and we are tempted to deal with them as if it were merely a matter of our own strength.

I want to tell you that it is not an easy thing to count on God. It's easy for us to print on our money, "In God We Trust," but what do you believe that means for us as a nation? What does it mean to trust God? Do you think our nation really does trust God? How many people do you meet in a day who really trust God? In the decision processes at work or at home, in your neighborhood, in the quietness of your own room, are you able to really trust God?

You see, a part of our problem is that we don't commit our mind to understanding God. We know what the second commandment in Exodus 20:4–5 says: "You shall not make for yourself an idol, whether in the form of anything that is in heaven above, or that is on the earth beneath, or that is in the water under the earth. You shall not bow down to them or worship them; for I the Lord your God am a jealous God." And we say, "Whoopee! We're not idolatrous. We figured out a long time ago that those idols are not God." Well, remember that Paul redefines the covetous person as an idolater (Eph. 5:5, KJV). Because, you see, anything that we trust in the physical realm and make ultimate becomes our god. If we live for that, if we count on that, it's our god.

George Fox, founder of the Quaker movement, was a great Christian. You may not agree with everything he said or did, but you would be challenged by reading his journal. There's a section in his journal where he talks about how this temptation beset him:

> One morning, as I was sitting by the fire, a great cloud came over me, and a temptation beset me; and I sat still. It was said, "All things come by nature"; and the elements and stars came over me, so that I was in a manner quite clouded with it. But as I sat still and said nothing, the people of the house perceived nothing. And as I sat still under it and let it alone, a living hope and a true voice arose in me, which said, "There is a living God who made all things." Immediately the cloud and temptation vanished away, and life rose over it all; my heart was glad, and I praised the living God. After some time I met with some people who had a notion that there was no God, but that all things come by nature. I had a great dispute with them, and overturned them, and made some of them confess that there is a living God. Then I saw that it was good that I had gone through that exercise. We had great meetings in those parts; for the power of the Lord broke through in that side of the country.[2]

"All things come by nature." That's the basic principle of idolatry. You see, if all things come by nature, then here you are in the middle of nature and you had better do something about it. So you will take things in your own hands and do as humanity has done ever since Babel. We're still in the business of trying to rise up and take over nature. The great Baconian statement "Knowledge is power" is our watchword, and now we've gone as far as putting our hand into the inner workings of the atom in the quest to dominate nature.

C. S. Lewis's *Abolition of Man* is a beautiful statement of what happens when humanity regards itself as being in the driver's seat.[3] We inevitably come to the place where, in order to dominate nature, we have to dominate—guess who?—humanity. And there's no escape in that logic.

So, you see, we're constantly in a bind. We have to deal with the physical world, don't we? We are in fact physical ourselves. We live in a body in the midst of a physical world. And the processes going on around us keep going. We have global warming, cell-phone radiation, and pesticides on our food. When I was a child in Missouri, one of my teachers told us that someday people would *pay* for drinking water. We thought that was the most ridiculous thing imaginable. Yet here we are. We are caught up in the physical realm.

Because of its massive presence, there's a great temptation to believe that the natural, physical world is all that exists. That idea has tremendous strength, and it is what lies behind the worldview that we have come rightly to characterize as a major tendency in our own culture—secular humanism. This is a belief that the natural world is "it." Period. And there isn't anything you can count on beyond the natural processes of this world. Secular humanism presents itself as things like separation of church and state or various issues in legal matters and rights.

WHY IS GOD NOT
MORE OBVIOUS?

If you're going to do apologetics in a way that is helpful for yourself and others, you're going to have to explain why God is not more obvious than he is. One of the reasons I often give to people is that *if God showed up in his full glory, we could all just kiss our free will good-bye.*

From the viewpoint of the natural world, God is not very obvious to those who do not wish to see him. I suppose he could write in the sky every morning what he wanted us to know for the day. That would be impressive, wouldn't it? He could have wired our minds so that he could directly communicate in an undeniable way with us every minute of the day. But none of this would be consistent with his project for humanity.

When God created human beings and gave them a job, which he did right off, he left some distance between them and himself. And he came to visit with them. From the very beginning God intended that we should have fellowship with him, but also that there should be some distance, so that we might be free and capable of choosing and deciding what we would be.

You have to face this with your children. If you had the power to completely control your children, I'm sure you would decide that you should not use that power most of the time. Once in a while, yes, but most of the time, no. This is because you know you would destroy your children. Children must choose. And to choose, they must have some distance, some freedom. Children must be able to do things without being known. And God chooses not to know everything.

GOD'S OMNISCIENCE

I get a lot of resistance to the idea that God can choose not to know things, because people are concerned about God's omniscience. But let me tell you that *God's omniscience does not overwhelm his omnipotence.* God does not have to know anything he does not wish to know. His omniscience refers to his *ability* to know everything, just as his omnipotence refers to his *ability* to do anything he wishes. God's omnipotence does not mean that he is always doing—or that he ever does—everything he *can* do. In the same way, he does not have to know everything he *can* know. He is capable of not knowing whatever he does not wish to know—should there be any such thing.

If God chooses to forget about my sins, he can do that. He doesn't have to stand there and stare at them eternally because I did them and he knows everything. The doctrine of God's omniscience is an expression of his omnipotence. That is to say, he *can* know anything he wants to; and anything he doesn't want to know he doesn't *have* to. And among the things that he chooses not to know are certain things about you and me.

Do you think God was playing a game when he came into the Garden and said to Adam, "Where are you?" (Gen. 3:9). I don't think he was. Our project in sin is to hide from God, but God is so big that, in order for us to hide from him, he must hide from us. If he doesn't hide from us, we're *sure* not going to be able to hide from him. And so God gives us space. This is for the purpose of allowing his redemptive act to approach us in history and allowing us to seek him and to find him. The scriptures tell us that if, with all our hearts, we seek him, we shall surely find him.

WHY IS THERE A HELL?

Some people not only want to hide from God, but want to be as far away from God as possible. Many people simply do not want to be with God. The best place for them to be is wherever God is not, and that's what hell is.[4] The fundamental reality of hell is separation from God, and that comes about because people do not want to be with him. For those people, being *with* God is the worst thing that could possibly happen to them.

A part of our problem with understanding hell comes from the way we think about heaven. We think about heaven as some kind of comfortable resort, but the greatest thing about heaven is going to be the presence of God. He has allowed us to avoid him here on earth in some measure if we want to, but if you go to heaven, God's the biggest thing on the horizon. You're no longer going to be able to avoid him. And that would be the supreme torture if you haven't gotten over thinking of *yourself* as God. That's why I sometimes say that the fires of heaven burn hotter than the fires of hell.

We have developed a great deal of symbolism about hell through the ages, even to the point of imagining what the furniture will be like. Some of this has really led us astray. For example, many people think the Devil is in charge of hell. He's often portrayed as the king there. But he is the one who is absolutely *not* in charge. He is at the receiving end of whatever there is in the way of punishment and suffering in hell. He's responsible for causing plenty of that in this world, but he is not responsible for what happens in hell.

Of course, it is not God's will that anyone should perish. God is not trying to keep people out of heaven. He's trying to get them *into* heaven. Some people think that God is sort of up there with his foot against the door, unwilling to let people in. Well, *he* is willing, but the issue is, can *you* stand to be there? And if you made it, would it be heaven to you, or would it be something much worse?

The only way it would be possible for there not to be a hell would be if everyone loved God, wanted him to be God, and wanted to be in his presence. Then it would not only be possible; it would be actual. We have people doing their best to make it work out that way. The Universalist point of view is that God is eventually going to work things out so that everyone gets into heaven. (That is not something we're in a position to assure anyone about, however.) And reincarnation is emerging today in some circles of Christianity to give us the opportunity to go around several times until we develop into the kind of people who actually love to be in the presence of God.

The human will is perhaps the one thing in the universe, because it is so precious and important, that God respects ultimately. C. S. Lewis wrote:

> *There are only two kinds of people in the end: those who say to God, "Thy will be done," and those to whom God says,*

in the end, "Thy will be done." All that are in Hell choose it.
Without that self-choice there could be no Hell. No soul that
seriously and constantly desires joy will ever miss it.[5]

God permits people to be away from him. If their hearts are really set on seeing themselves as God and they are intent on running their own world, that will keep them away from God. This is like the teacher who finally sends the trouble-making student out of the classroom, as it were, and says, "Okay, if you want to go away, you can go away."

Jesus was constantly trying to enfold people in his kingdom. He was not trying to send people to hell; he was trying to get as many people into heaven as he could. We need to understand that's where God's heart is. I used to work in Texas with a minister who said, "God's gonna skip them sinners across the lake of fire like a boy skips a rock across a lake." Can you imagine that? But that's where our images can go wrong. The Reformer John Calvin (1509–64) had some wonderful things to say about how, in communicating with us in reference to these ultimate things, God does the best he can within the limitations of our imagination and thought.

But sometimes those images go wild, and we wind up with the wrong impression of God. I often deal with people who have a difficult time processing the images of God in the Old Testament especially. My constant word to them is simply to listen to what Jesus said about God. He is the one who said, "Whoever has seen me has seen the Father" (John 14:9). Now, that's the saving thought in this discussion. It tells you where the heart of God is.

God did *not* create hell because he's mad, he wants to see people suffer, and he enjoys torturing them for eternity. The only reason there is a hell is because God makes provision for what people want, and hell is simply the best God can do for some people.

"THEY ARE WITHOUT EXCUSE"

God gives us space, so we can hide. He doesn't run over us. And as a result, the physical world stands there, from the unredeemed point of view, as being all the reality there is. But it isn't! And although God is not obvious, he is inevitable. An acquaintance of mine, Dr. A. E. Wilder-Smith, wrote a book called *He Who Thinks Has to Believe*.[6] Of course, we can choose not to think, but *if* we think, he maintains, we will believe in God. Notice Paul's word on that in Romans 1:19–20:

> For what can be known about God is plain to them, because God has shown it to them. Ever since the creation of the world his eternal power and divine nature, invisible though they are, have been understood and seen through the things he has made. So they are without excuse.

Look at those verses carefully in view of these points. There is a tradition within evangelical theology and the training of the ministry that says something to the effect that there is no common ground upon which believers and unbelievers meet. You will have a note on Genesis 1:1 in some of your study Bibles that says something like, "The Bible never argues for

God." Those kinds of statements need to come to terms with these verses from Paul. Other statements, such as Psalm 19, also clearly indicate that there is an evidential process that is so clear and so forceful that it leaves every person without excuse. So we're going to look at this argument, spell it out, and try to make it as clear as possible.

WHY THE PHYSICAL WORLD CANNOT BE ALL THERE IS

Put on your logical hats now, and let's go through this carefully. I believe we can make the heart of the argument obvious, and that will take us back to Romans 1:20. We are now spelling out what it is about the creation of the world that makes us see that there is an invisible eternal God. The bottom line in the discussion of creation is: Do we live in a world that runs on its own or not? I believe that it is by far the most reasonable to believe in a personal being of unlimited power as the reason for the condition of the natural world.

The first thing we observe when we look around in the physical world is that every event—every physical event, every natural event—depends on something other than itself. Each event has a cause. You cannot find a case where that is not true, no matter how far you expand your attention in time or space. No matter how you cut it up, every way of articulating the physical world leaves the parts dependent on something outside of themselves and indeed before themselves. Now, the causal theories behind any event you may wish to pick out—

for example, you are reading these words right now; that's an event—are complete at the point where the event occurred. It's important to understand what that means: that means all of the causes leading up to your reading this page have happened. That series is finished. No more causes are going to occur. We're not waiting for any of them to occur, because it's all over and done with and if it had not been over and done with, you would not be reading these words.

You can write science-fiction stories about the space-time continuum and how various segments might intersect with one another, or you can make movies as if an event in this point in time was still waiting on causes that come after it, but fiction is not reality. Don't try to get anyone to believe that the causes of any *real* event are still waiting to happen. They will simply not accept it—and for good reason. Since that series is completed, it is finite. That is to say, it is not infinitely long. It may be very long, and when we talk about creation, we're certain it is *extremely* long. You can argue about "old earth" and "new earth," but even with "new earth" the series is *very* long. But it's *finite*. If it were not finite, there would be an uncountably large number of causes in the series, so that if you start anywhere, as far back as you can go, and come forward as far as you can go, you will *never* exhaust the causes.

THE PHYSICAL CAUSES FOR ANY EVENT CANNOT BE INFINITE

If you have an infinitely long chain of dominoes and you tip the one near the back—remember, there are an infinite number of dominoes in between—what will happen to the ones up in front? They will never fall. Because no matter how many dominoes were knocked down, there will still be more to knock down. You will never get to the final domino if it has a series of infinite causes behind it. You see? That means that the series of causes must have a first member that is itself self-subsistent, and so not a physical or natural event or thing.

By self-subsistent being I merely mean something that doesn't depend on anything else for its existence: a mind, a will, which has its existence entirely within itself. Many people say, "Wait a minute, there can't be anything like that!" But that is merely a reflection of our submersion in things that are all dependent upon something else for their existence. We are so used to thinking of only physical and finite things, that the very idea of a self-subsistent being seems strange to us, even though that is what is constantly presented to us in the scriptures.

In Exodus 3:14, when Moses asks God for his name and God responds, "I am that I am" (KJV) this is God's way of saying he has always been and always will be. He is infinite and self-subsistent. In John 5:26, we find Jesus talking the same way as he is teaching about his power to call even those who are dead to life. He says, "As the Father has life in himself . . ." ("life in himself"—that is self-subsistent being) ". . . so he has granted the Son also to have life in himself." And we see the generosity of the triune God sharing between the persons in the unity of one substantial self-subsistent being: the personal reality that underlies all of creation.

As in the case of those dominoes, the first member that lies at the basis of the physical series of causation—the one who tipped the domino—cannot be physical itself, because it is not itself dependent on something other than itself. And in the same way, we reach the conclusion that *creation of the physical world rests upon something without a cause outside of itself, a first cause that, in relation to nature, is supernatural and self-subsistent.*

Now, those of you who have taken a little philosophy of religion or otherwise thought about this will know that there are a lot of different ways of trying to circumvent this, and I have not, by any means, touched on all of them. I think one of the best atheistic representations, on the other side, is in a book by J. L. Mackie called *The Miracle of Theism.*[7] However you try to deal with this argument, you will find that it indeed represents a very good demonstration of this conclusion.

You may be inclined to say we've still gained nothing with this, because it doesn't prove that God exists. Be patient. Take each piece out of the segments of the argument that present themselves and then move on to further reasoning. But you must understand that just this part of the argument alone is very important in the modern context, where the driving attitude of atheistic thought is *always* to reduce reality to the natural world. To have an argument that shows that this is impossible and *there must have been some form of self-subsistent being beforehand* is a great step forward and, for all practical purposes, undermines atheism in its modern form. Atheism in its modern form is always naturalistic and physicalistic, so to have shown that the world cannot be understood that way is a considerable attainment.

COMMONPLACE MYTHS OF THE "BIG BANG" AND OF "COSMIC EVOLUTION"

Let's quickly add one additional point now, because thus far nothing has been said about the nature of this self-subsistent being. Where does order come from in a world such as ours? Some of you who follow cosmological speculation will know that quite a discussion began in the 1980s about how, if the universe was a uniform kind of quark soup after the big bang, order could have emerged in it such as we have—especially when we look at the various great walls of galaxies, which seem totally incomprehensible from the viewpoint of cosmic evolution as we've understood it.

There are two major myths about how the universe got started. One is the big-bang theory, and the other is the cosmic-evolution theory. The big-bang theory functions as a myth because no one attempts to explain the big bang; that's not regarded as a problem. This is always the mark of a myth. A myth shows up when we need to explain something that is functioning, but no one knows how it actually works.

What is actually presumed by any working cosmologist I know is that the big bang is most certainly *not* the origin of the universe. There was a highly compressed point of matter and energy (you get various descriptions, because they don't really know how to describe it) that exploded. You can't get a scientist to talk in terms of *nothing* banging. No *real scientist* will do that. Nor will any scientist try to convince you, strictly speaking, that order can come out of disorder.

Physical stuff is essentially the kind of thing that comes from something else. We don't just say, "We have these wonderful things here, and they came from nothing." Sometimes I tell my students that I'm giving them copies of a paper for which there is no original. That usually makes the point.

When you are dealing with people who believe in a big-bang theory, that the universe came from nothing, ask them to show you a peer-review journal or a professionally vetted textbook that explains how that happened. Ask them where to find one. That is one way you can help people think about this seriously.

The myth of cosmic evolution is that order comes out of disorder. That's the only way atheists can avoid the assumption that not only is there a self-subsistent being, but this self-subsistent being is a great mind that *knows*. You see, from antiquity on, people have said, "Obviously there must be a God because of the order in the cosmos. Obviously there must be!" The suggestion of cosmic evolution as an alternative was not presented until the nineteenth century. It involves this curious difficulty that evolution cannot account for order, because it always *presupposes* order. Evolution is something that occurs to entities of a specific kind in a specifically structured environment. You cannot get evolution unless you already have order.

ORDER COMES FROM MINDS

The one place we know order comes from is minds. Nearly everything you see around you, except you, was produced by a mind. We constantly experience order coming from human minds into physical reality, whether it is chocolate cakes, space shuttles, or computers. Now, it's been proven that there is a preexisting material that minds work on, but we all know that those things causally depend upon minds conceiving them and fashioning them. And we have experience that would lead us not to believe anything else about order generally.

A creative mind lies behind the physical world. You can read all about that in the first chapter of Genesis. And read again in Romans 1 these words from Paul: "Ever since the creation of the world his eternal power and divine nature, invisible though they are, have been understood and seen through the things he has made. So they are without excuse." And Hebrews 11:3: "By faith we understand that the worlds were prepared by the word of God, so that what is seen [the creation] was made from things that are not visible." Relative to our data, then, we must believe that the first cause of physical reality would also be a mind, and a sufficiently great mind at that.

READING E = MC² FROM
LEFT TO RIGHT

The interrelationship of energy and mass is a fundamental point to understand for theology. We, as human beings, always read $E = mc^2$ from right to left. We've got this mass of stuff, and we'd like to turn it into energy to run generators or blow something up. There are actually accelerators, such as the Large Hadron Collider near Geneva, Switzerland, that have been created to try to get particles up to enough speed, so that when they collide they will have enough energy to create matter. Now, God doesn't have any problem with this. He is infinite energy. Notice that I didn't say he *has* infinite energy. I said he *is* infinite energy. And his word goes forth in his actions to create matter. And every bit of matter that you see, including your body, is held together by God's act.

Four passages of scripture are especially useful when you study the action of God sustaining every physical reality:

> Hebrews 1:2–3: "He sustains all things by his powerful word . . ."
>
> Colossians 1:16–17: "In him all things in heaven and on earth were created . . ."
>
> 2 Peter 3:10–11: "All these things are to be dissolved . . ."
>
> Acts 17:28: "In him we live and move and have our being . . ."

It's important not to just say that there must be such a being as God to bring our universe into existence, but to have some conceptualization of what's involved. Scripture talks about this in many, many cases. For example, Paul in Colossians 1:16 gives us a wonderful statement about creation: "In him all things in heaven and on earth were created, things visible and invisible, whether thrones or dominions or rulers or powers." Then Paul continues in verse 17: "He himself is before all things, and in him all things hold together." Everything hangs together in him. The other end of that is in 2 Peter 3:10 with this wonderful statement about the end times: "The day of the Lord will come like a thief, and then the heavens will pass away with a loud noise, and the elements will be dissolved with fire." The word translated *dissolved* is *duromenone,* which really means *turned loose.* Everything will be turned loose, come apart, dissolve.

Once you understand this, you're prepared to get very serious about God's relation to the physical universe, and then issues like miracles and so on fit in very nicely. When Jesus turned the water into wine (John 2:1–11), he just readjusted his hold on the matter that made up the water. I have a chemist friend who says this couldn't have happened, because the heat and energy required for such a transformation would have blown the place apart. But we're talking about the one who knows how it all fits together—who knows how to handle those little contingencies. And when you see the waves responding to his words (Mark 4:35–41), they're responding to the one who holds them together anyway.

Out of the infinite energy of the personal, self-subsistent God, matter coalesces, along with his purposes, in the creation of the physical universe. Keep in mind that the physical universe is not all he created. When we read Genesis 1:1, it says, "In the beginning when God created the heavens"—plural— "and the earth." But we sort of zip by the heavens and focus on the earth as if that's all that really matters. The earth is a very small part of creation, and we want to keep that in mind.

I'm not trying to do armchair science by bringing up $E = mc^2$. I'm just saying this is our best knowledge, and it really fits in well with what the scriptures tell us. Once we learn to read that equation from left to right as well as from right to left, it helps us understand that God's action transforms his energy into matter (Gen. 1; Heb. 11:3). That's the nice thing about equations—they work in both directions.

GOD'S INVOLVEMENT IN SCIENCE AND TECHNOLOGY

I praise God for science. I believe it is his work. If you know the history of science, you must agree that it's of God, because human beings are just staggering through it. It may interest you to look at Arthur Koestler's book *The Sleepwalkers*,[8] in which he discusses many of the great figures in the rise of modern science. The "reconciliation" of science and the Bible is a serious task, because they are both so fundamental to humankind's call to be responsible children of God. Scientific hypotheses are held tentatively, whereas biblical truth is eternal. It is not necessary to have total reconciliation of the two, yet some amount of harmony is required. And understanding their interrelations is not easy. I truly believe that God's hand is in history in the form of the development of technology and science. I believe it is a part of his plan to approach us through human history, and I think there will be science and technology in heaven too.

I'm thankful for the scientific advances we have seen in our day, because I am sure that the more we learn, the more we're going to be assured that, indeed, what the Bible says about creation and physical reality is true. I'm sure of it, and I can't wait. That won't solve all of our problems, but I believe what Paul said in Romans 1:19–20: "For what can be known about God is plain to them, because God has shown it to them. Ever since the creation of the world his eternal power and divine nature, invisible though they are, have been understood and seen through the things he has made. So they are without excuse."

This is still true in the age of the Hubble space telescope and will continue to be ever more clearly true.

FAITH TO BUILD YOUR LIFE ON

We don't have to look very far into our own thinking and living to see the effects of either being sure of God or not being sure of God. I believe that scripture always presents real faith as something that is based on knowledge as well as something that goes beyond anything you could know, and involves a commitment to God and his kingdom. Those two things, knowledge and commitment, are not exclusive of one another; rather, they are related. If we do not have a knowledge of God at the foundation of our commitment, that commitment simply will not hold up. It will waver; it will not govern our lives. It will be like pulling a chair away from someone in the act of sitting down. We will not be able to hold on to our belief as God intends, by the action of his Spirit on our hearts and our minds.

Knowledge and faith are intended to go together. For example, when you read Hebrews 11, the great chapter on faith, you will see faith equated with a vision of reality. We are told that Moses endured as one who sees the invisible. Faith is not a mere thought that something is true or the hope or resolve to believe it is. As Martin Luther said in the preface to his commentary on Romans:

Faith is a living, well-founded confidence in the grace of God, so perfectly certain that it would die a thousand times rather than surrender its conviction. Such confidence and personal knowledge of divine grace makes its possessor joyful, bold, and full of warm affection toward God and all created things—all of which the Holy Spirit works in faith. Hence, such a man becomes without constraint willing and eager to do good to everyone, to serve everyone, to suffer all manner of ills, in order to please and to glorify God, who has shown toward him such grace. It is thus impossible to separate works from faith—yea, just as impossible as to separate burning and shining from fire.[9]

So when we contrast faith and sight, we always have to be sure that we qualify it, so that we understand what kind of sight we are talking about. And that kind of sight—the vision of the self-subsistent being without which all of the universe as we know it would simply fold up and disappear—that knowledge, that faith, that vision is the rock upon which we can build our lives.

Chapter Five

COMMUNICATION
BETWEEN GOD
AND HUMANITY

*Then I saw a new heaven and a new earth; for the first
heaven and the first earth had passed away, and the sea
was no more. And I saw the holy city, the new Jerusalem,
coming down out of heaven from God, prepared as a bride
adorned for her husband.*

REVELATION 21:1–2

*Nothing accursed will be found there any more. But the
throne of God and of the Lamb will be in it, and his servants will worship him; they will see his face, and his name
will be on their foreheads. And there will be no more night;
they need no light of lamp or sun, for the Lord God will be
their light, and they will reign for ever and ever.*

REVELATION 22:3–5

83

As we move in apologetic work beyond the issue of God's existence and basic nature, our work becomes less a matter of proof, though that remains absolutely crucial at certain points, and more a matter of "making sense" of the elements of Christian faith, showing that of course it would be such as it is.

We are now at the point where we want to deal with questions that arise about the choice of a covenant people of God in history and about the Bible. I am not going to start out with the standard routine of trying to prove to you that the Bible is true and dealing with all of the objections. The reason for that is very simple. When we get to this point in developing an apologetic in the manner that I believe Christians should, it is more important to make sense of our faith than to try to prove things to people (especially those who do not want to believe them anyway). We need to show that having a Bible like the one we do is exactly the right thing, if one intends what God intends to do with human beings in history. We need to show that calling an individual, Abraham, making him your friend, and calling his family to be a light to all the earth is exactly the sort of thing that you would do if you intended to accomplish in human history what God intends to accomplish. So we are going to be looking at those things pretty carefully now.

As we move into the more particular issues about a covenant people, the discussion is going to extend in a different way to the church itself and the book of God that came from that tradition. Now, remember that our aim is to work with reason and the Spirit to resolve doubts and enhance confidence in God's presence in our lives—the God presented in the Bible—in such a way that it causes people to inquire about what you have in your life and what makes you the way you are. Those people need to receive an answer from us that will help them come to have that same faith.

We do not suppose that we are going to convert people or change their lives merely by the power of our own reasoning. But, as with everything in life, we are called by God to put forth our efforts in expectation and faith that they will be anointed and that in the effect of those efforts we will see a greater difference than we could possibly make on our own. The mark of the Spirit in an activity is always the incommensurability of the result with the effort. Always. And if you look through the Bible or listen to the testimonies of Christians, you will see that that is the way it always works. We put forth our effort, and the result is much greater than could possibly be caused by our effort alone.

Remember that in doing the work of apologetics, we are helping Christians and non-Christians. This includes ourselves as well as others, because if the medicine we have isn't good for us, it probably won't be good for others. We are using our reason to help people come to a clear place of faith, where their confidence in the God of the Bible will be just as real as the floor on which they stand. That's faith. That's the kind of faith that results in peace, hope, and obedience, because it is a faith that puts us in touch with the reality of the kingdom of God.

Thus far we have worked through basic arguments about the reality of God. We went over the argument that proves that there must exist an infinite, self-subsistent, personal being and without it nothing physical would exist. We talked about why God is not obvious, why he allows there to be a world that seems to run on its own until you begin to dig into it to try to find out what makes it work and how it could possibly exist.

Now we want to move on from there and ask ourselves questions about how that being relates to this world. We are going to follow the analogy of God to human beings as creator to creations, and we are going to need to draw some other truths out of that comparison. In other words, we need to think at greater length about how a mind relates to its creations. In order to understand how the reasoning works, we have to divide the evidence we look to in understanding the Christian faith into three levels. The first level is the level of history.

THE PROCESS OF CREATION

We need to look carefully at what has actually happened to human beings in the course of our history here on the earth. When we think about that, we might want to ask ourselves what it is that would make us think that God has a continuing interest in human beings. In order to get the answer, we have to go back to the act of creation and the whole idea of creating something.

How do you generally feel about the things you create? If you make a peanut-butter sandwich for someone, and that person puts it on the ground and steps on it, how do you feel? You see, we have a continuing interest in what we create. And that's characteristic of all forms of creation. Even if it is a botched job, we have a continuing interest in it, which is why we may even feel ashamed of it. We are not simply indifferent to it.

There is always a sustained relationship between creator and creation, whether it is you and the peanut-butter sandwich or God and his world. Because in the process of creation, we impart the substance of ourselves into what we create. Perhaps a peanut-butter sandwich doesn't call for much, but after all you did invest your choice, thought, and energy into making that sandwich. And that's why you are not indifferent about what happens to it. What happens to that sandwich genuinely matters to you. Even if you were to say, "Well, I'm silly to let it matter!" it still matters.

As we continue with the analogy of creator to creature and of human mind to its inventions, what we see is that God has a continuing interest in his creation. And like all of those who create anything at all, the primary part of the image of God in human beings is creative action. When you go back to Genesis 1, you will see that the story runs directly from "Let us make humankind in our image" to "let them have dominion" (v. 26).

God created us and gave us a body, so that we would have an independent power source for action. That is what your body is: your independent power source. It is the little "power pack" that God has assigned to each of us for use in our freedom and development. God built it to work in such a way that we can even use it to rebel against him. When we look at our own creative capacities, how we relate to the things that we make, we see a structure that is common to God and his creation as well as to us and our creations. What that means is that we create for good, and God creates for good.

Now, this is an analogical argument, so it is not an argument that intends to be deductively valid. A deductively valid argument is one in which, if the premises are true, it is absolutely necessary that the conclusion be true. Analogical reasoning is more like a standard of what's reasonable to accept. For example, if you look at the tall buildings in downtown Los Angeles, those were planned and built using analogical reasoning, usually on actuarial tables. Now, deductively that is not a valid argument. It is an argument that proceeds by suggesting a similar circumstance from a similar situation. So this kind of an argument has to be appraised in terms of that sort of structure.[1] When you appraise an analogical argument, you look to see how strong the comparison is.

Obviously there are some differences in this analogy. For example, God created matter out of nothing, and we certainly can't do that. We never create peanut-butter sandwiches out of nothing. We create them out of bread and peanut butter. Nonetheless, if you look at the creative process itself, it will bear the conclusion that a creative mind cares about what happens to its product. This is especially true the better the creator is in mind and character.

Now, sometimes we do things that are evil. But even then there is some good in view as far as we are *subjectively* concerned. We are pursuing something of value even when we don't realize that it is a wrong value. When God creates, he creates for good. He comes to make something that is good, and because of that, he continues to have an interest in it, he continues to work with it, and he continues to care for it; that is a part of the structure of all creative action.

So the first truth we want to try to make stand out as clearly as possible in this line of reasoning is that there is a good purpose to human history and the individual life therein: to develop and contribute to a glorious, triumphant community of unqualified love, understanding, and freedom. God has continuing interaction with his creation to see to it that good comes of it.

BUILDING ON WHAT'S ALREADY BEEN ESTABLISHED

We must keep the previous stages of the argument in mind here. One of the mistakes often made in apologetics is that we don't keep things in order as we move along. So when we come to this point we must be mindful that we are not trying to establish that there is a God. Nor are we trying to establish that there is a God with a personality. That has already been established. Now our question is: *Given that there is such a God, what are we to make of human history?* We must always keep that in mind. If you don't keep things carefully in order, many issues in apologetics will just wipe you out.

For example, one of the main problems in apologetics is the existence of evil. Why do evil and suffering exist in the world? Many people approach that question without any evidence that God already exists, and as a result they are totally incapable of dealing with it, because they cannot bring before them a large enough view of reality to enable them to work on this difficult question. You must already have dealt with the question of God's existence first, so that when you come to a serious issue like evil you are not asking, "Does God exist?" Rather, you are asking, "Given that God exists, how are we to understand the presence of evil in the world?"

And so it is when we think about human history. It is always important to remember that we are not looking at history as if it were something we just discovered for the first time, so that we ask, "What's this?" We come having already established that there is an infinite, self-subsistent, personal being that created human history. And when we look at it from that point of view, the key to understanding is the realization that there is some good purpose to human history.

Now let's belabor that a bit. There really is some good purpose to human history. Why should I say such a thing as that? Let's go back over it and exercise our *reason:*

1. Human history is the result of a personal God, who is its creator.

2. Creators create for good.

3. Human history is created.

Therefore: Human history is created for good.

Now, one of the things you learn in doing apologetics is to try to state these kinds of arguments as clearly and formally as possible. Then you can begin to delve into the issues. And if you have questions in your mind about those premises I just listed, I hope you will write them down and work with them until you begin to get some satisfaction concerning them. Remember that they come out of the analogy between God as creator and anyone as creator.

GOD'S GOOD PURPOSES
IN HUMAN HISTORY

When we look at human history now, our question is: What could the good purpose in human history be? But one of the things that bothers people when they take this question up is, "How do I know that God is good at all?" I will tell you very simply how I know that God is good. If he were not good, if he were evil, the world would have been so much worse than it is. This assures me that he could not possibly be evil. I mean, we need to think about how bad it *could* be. Suppose the world were one large concentration camp? We will deal with evil more extensively in the next chapter, but my point to you here is that we have a good God who is opposed to evil.

The scriptural view is that God is constantly guarding against evil, that he constantly struggles with the evil in the world. You find this stated over and over throughout scripture. For example, in Genesis 6, before the flood, God says, "My spirit shall not always strive with man, for that he also is flesh:

yet his days shall be an hundred and twenty years" (v. 3, KJV). That is a picture of God striving with the evil that is in the heart of humankind and restraining it. In fact, in that passage, it looks as if God decided to shorten the life span of human beings to limit the time they can resist God. You see, the Spirit of God is constantly present in human life.

Think a moment about Job. Job is an interesting person to consider in connection with these topics, because he was not a member of the covenant people. Job was not a Jew, but God had a hedge around Job. And instead of thinking of Job as an exception, I want you to think about Job as the rule. God places a hedge around all of those who seek him, preventing evil from happening to them. You remember that Jeremiah in Lamentations 3:22 says it is through "the Lord's mercies that we are not consumed" (KJV).

There's an old hymn called "Great Is Thy Faithfulness." I hope you know the chorus:

> *Great is Thy faithfulness,*
> *Great is Thy faithfulness,*
> *Morning by morning,*
> *New mercies I see.*[2]

Are those just pretty words? Many things in our Bible and in our songs have become a series of pretty words that don't really mean anything to us anymore. There is so much in the Bible about God's resistance to evil. Don't miss it.

In 2 Thessalonians 2:6–8, Paul is talking to the Thessalonians about the coming of the antichrist. He tells them that the antichrist will not come yet, because the one who is restraining evil has not yet been removed. There will come a time when the one who is restraining evil will be removed. In Galatians, we find Paul talking about how the spirit and the flesh are constantly struggling with one another (5:17). In Revelation 12:12, we see a time after Satan has been defeated in heaven and is thrown down upon the earth and the sea. There is mention of what it is going to be like when Satan has great force and power: he is angry and frightened because, as scripture says there, his time is short.

In the Lord's Prayer, we are taught, "Do not put us to the test, but deliver us from evil." What do you think that means? It means that we are to constantly ask for the protection of God against evil. We are on a battlefield. It is as if there are two armies, one of good and one of evil, and we are in the middle. But Satan cannot do anything about God; he is far too big. And Satan has a limited sphere of activity within which the only way he can get at God is to do evil to God's creatures.

I'm saying all of this to you because evil is real. And we have to understand that. We also need to know that God is against it and that he has set the means in place to protect us. God's angels are all around us. Jesus says in Matthew 18:10, when he is warning against offending little children, "Their angels continually see the face of my Father in heaven." *Their angels.* Jesus was very concerned about little children. He knows the terrible things that can happen to them. They are so precious to God that his care is over every one of them. Now, when children grow up and become old and ugly, like I am, maybe the angels just walk off. Do you think that's how it works? Well, I believe that they stay right there. God resists evil. He is not the author of it. He stands against it. We are in the arena of human history, in which the *good* purposes of God are to be accomplished.

Let's look just a moment at the way Paul states those purposes. Ephesians has a discussion about this conflict and the spirit that now works in the children of disobedience:

> But God, who is rich in mercy, out of the great love
> with which he loved us even when we were dead
> through our trespasses, made us alive together with
> Christ—by grace you have been saved—and raised us up
> with him and seated us with him in the heavenly places
> in Christ Jesus, so that in the ages to come he might
> show the immeasurable riches of his grace in kindness
> toward us in Christ Jesus. (2:4–7)

Now, *this* is what human history is about! (You'll have a lot of fascinating conversations if you can get people to tell you their view of what human history is about, by the way, especially if they happen to be atheists.) Look again at Paul's statement in verse 7: "That in the ages to come he might show the immeasurable riches of his grace in kindness toward us in Christ Jesus." You see, we are his showpieces who "in the ages to come" will be the evidence of his grace and kindness. And again in Ephesians 3:10:

> So that through the church the wisdom of God in its
> rich variety might now be made known to the rulers
> and authorities in the heavenly places.

What is to be made known is what God is going to bring out of human history, what Malachi 3:17 describes as his "jewels" (KJV).

What God is going to bring out of human history in his people is going to be the greatest reflection of God's own glory, wisdom, and love. That is what human history is about. It is to make a society of the redeemed that will be the crown jewel of creation. And when we look at all of the terrible things that happen in human history, when we look at the extent of human evil in it, we want to remember what would be lost if human history had not happened. What would be lost is precisely this crown jewel of creation, which consists of Christlike people living together with the kind of love that the members of the Trinity have for one another and enjoying that full, shared, self-subsistent being that characterizes God himself as God dwells in those people.

It's a little hard to paint a picture of this that does justice to it. But remember, that's what we are called to do. That's what the church at large is about. It is collecting those people, bringing them together, ministering to them, and calling others in to be a part of that great society of God that we must believe is the only way in which God can express the fullness of his glory, goodness, and greatness. *You* are a part of that. You share in that. And now, when an individual comes along and says to you, "Why are you so happy even though you are suffering? Why are you so happy when things go wrong? Where does the strength that is in you come from? Why is it that you have in you a life that flows out to others and words that change their lives?" you can say it is because God is present in human history through you and your community of fellowship. You can tell that individual, "This is what creation, reality, human life, and human history are all about."

You are probably still going to have a lot of work to do, but that is the core of the answer, and we must never lose sight of it. Even the angels seem not to understand it. We read in 1 Peter 1:12, as Peter is speaking of redemption and the gospel, that these are things "into which angels long to look." We believe that there will come a time when they will see the result and say, "Oh, *that* is what it was all about! That is why he created them! That is why he let them live in circumstances in which they could do wrong, and why he lived through a covenant people for many, many centuries and finally sent his own son to be rejected by those very covenant people, that he might create out of that a larger community of the redeemed." And they will know more fully the greatness and goodness of God.

If you were God, and you wished to accomplish this in human history, what would you do to bring it about? Remember, this is not something you can do just by rewiring people. Jesus said to those who criticized him in his day, "God is able from these stones to raise up children to Abraham" (Matt. 3:9). But he didn't, did he? Why wouldn't God have just directly created the community that we were talking about a moment ago? It is because in doing what he is doing in history, he is creating a community of love that freely responds to him, that *chooses* to be his, that diligently *seeks* until it finds him, and that finds in him the fullness of life. No robots here. No machines. Just people who have experienced free development of Christ-like character. Redeemed people.

THE FRIEND OF GOD

So when God went into human history, he found one man. I don't think this means that everyone else was untouched by him, but that when he came to accomplish these specific purposes, he chose one specific person—Abraham. The scriptural term for the relationship between Abraham and God is "friend." Abraham was the friend of God. Look with me at a few verses about this relationship, and then I hope you will look up other scriptures about Abraham and trace this friendship throughout the Bible on your own.

In a prayer at a time of national crisis for the people of Israel, Jehoshaphat says, "Did you not, O our God, drive out the inhabitants of this land before your people Israel, and give it for ever to the descendants of your *friend* Abraham?" (2 Chron. 20:7). Isaiah uses the same word in 41:8, "But you, Israel, my servant, Jacob, whom I have chosen, the offspring of Abraham, my *friend*," and spells out Abraham's calling in 42:5–7:

> Thus says God, the Lord, who created the heavens and stretched them out, who spread out the earth and what comes from it, who gives breath to the people upon it and spirit to those who walk in it: I am the Lord, I have called you in righteousness, I have taken you by the hand and kept you; I have given you as a covenant to the people, a light to the nations, to open the eyes that are blind, to bring out the prisoners from the dungeon, from the prison those who sit in darkness.

Notice how God is identified: "the Lord, who created the heavens, . . . who spread out the earth." That is always the way God is identified first and foremost in scripture. The second way he is identified is as one who had a covenant with Abraham: "I have given you as a covenant to the people, a light to the nations." The basic idea is that, because of the purposes God had for human history, when he got ready to approach humankind, he did so through an individual whom he made his friend; through the family of that individual, he created a people and a culture.

THE UNIQUENESS OF JEWISH CULTURE

We need to spend some time thinking about the Jews as a people. There are no people on earth like the Jews. They owe their existence for millennia up to the present to God alone and to the truth that God gave to them in their history and in their laws, which have been incorporated into a book. The highest iteration of God that has ever been given to humanity is in the Old Testament. And the New Testament, once you understand the Old, is simply a natural consequence.

Compare Psalm 23 to all other religious literature. You will see that it is not something that could have been made up. It is too *strange* to have been made up. And if you look at all the theories of the origin of religions with people like the philosopher David Hume or the psychologist Sigmund Freud, you won't find anything that accounts for the content of the Old Testament as expressed at its highest in Psalm 23. *You won't find anything.* Read Buddhist literature, read Hindu literature. Don't *talk* about them, *read* them. A lot of people read a verse or two, a passage or two, a sermon here or there from one of the other religions and assume that it fully represents that religion. No, read the whole thing and *then* compare them. You are going to find that there is no possibility of explaining the origination of the revelation and the teaching of the Jewish religion by natural principles.

ANIMAL SACRIFICE

Now, there are things in the history of Jewish culture that people struggle with. One in particular is the gruesome ritual of animal sacrifice. God gives very careful instructions on how and why specific sacrifices are to be made, and reading through them can be quite painful for those of us in our culture who support animal rights and welcome the tagline, "No animals were harmed in the making of this film." Along with annual festivals that require sacrifices from the Israelite families, occasions are recorded in scripture during which hundreds of animals were slaughtered for burnt offerings. What does this show us about the God we say is so good and loving?

This is a reflection of the way God meets people where they are. He is willing to make concessions to the people he is trying to communicate with, and he will redeem them through the reality of their circumstances. The culture of the ancient world was a violent one in many ways, and animal sacrifices were a regular part of how business was done. When you made an agreement with someone, you didn't just shake hands and sign on the dotted line. In those days, you "cut" a covenant with the other party. That meant you cut animals in half and walked between the pieces together, which basically said, "May what has happened to these animals happen to anyone who breaks this agreement." So God used sacrifices because it was something the people understood. God is not a snob who requires us to get everything right before he'll have anything to do with us. His willingness to meet us where we are is crucial to his project of redeeming us.

Animal sacrifices began when the first humans sinned. Some animals had to give up their skin to cover the nakedness that was revealed when people stopped trusting God (Gen. 3:21). They didn't need clothes before that. The Bible doesn't say why this is so, but I believe it was because they glowed. When you look at a lightbulb, the light is so bright you can't actually see the bulb. Because of the glow, Adam and Eve couldn't tell whether they were naked or not, and so they didn't need any clothes. Sin has us running on very low wattage now, but I believe we will glow again when we are perfected in Christ. Sometimes you see people who glow a little more than usual—someone who is in love or someone who is a new grandparent. We call them "radiant." There's extra power coming through. And when we are plugged in to God, the same power comes through, because radiance is a manifestation of energy.

Also, we're apt to overlook the fact that at the time God gave instruction regarding animal sacrifice, there was no class of clergy and intellectuals. The function of the sacrificial system was to provide a way of living for a class of people (priests) who were not working the farm. If that had not been established, there would have been no growth of language, of the Bible as we know it, of Jewish history, and there would never have come a time when a little town of Bethlehem could appear and Jesus could come into this world as a baby, grow up as a human being, and have the effect he has had on this world. So animal sacrifice was a way for God to meet people where they were and work through human history to bring about his purposes in the world.

GOD WORKS WITHIN
THE CULTURE

When God brought the Israelites out of Egypt, they were the lowest socioeconomic class imaginable. Human life was basically worthless in that culture, and the individual did not stand out as something to be cared for. That is why we read about laws of corporate responsibility in the Old Testament. If a man did something wrong, it was the cultural norm for his whole family to be killed and his house made into a dung heap.

The story of Achan in Joshua 7 is a perfect example. The first verse tells us that Achan (just one man) "took some of the devoted things" home with him from the battle of Jericho, "and the anger of the Lord burned against the Israelites" (the whole nation). God's instructions for taking the city of Jericho included keeping "away from the things devoted to destruction, so as not to covet and take any of the devoted things and make the camp of Israel an object for destruction, bringing trouble upon it" (6:18). No one knew what Achan had done, but when Joshua sent soldiers to their next battle, at the city of Ai, what should have been an easy victory ended in defeat. Joshua went to the Lord about this, and the Lord replied:

> Stand up! Why have you fallen upon your face? Israel
> has sinned; they have transgressed my covenant that I

imposed on them. They have taken some of the devoted things; they have stolen, they have acted deceitfully, and they have put them among their own belongings. Therefore the Israelites are unable to stand before their enemies; they turn their backs to their enemies, because they have become a thing devoted for destruction themselves. I will be with you no more, unless you destroy the devoted things from among you. (7:10–12)

So they drew lots and discovered that Achan had taken a Babylonian robe, five pounds of silver, and a bar of gold and hidden it all underneath his tent. The punishment for this was that Achan and his entire family were taken to the valley of Achor, where they were *all* stoned to death and then burned with all their belongings. Since we read about this in the Bible, we automatically assume that this is a punishment dictated by God. But this was a cultural norm at that time throughout the known world. Later on God makes it clear that corporate responsibility is not a good thing of which he approves. But he didn't jump in and change things on the spot because of the course of human development in history as well as in individuals.

God uses history to allow people to approach him in a way that will not consume them. He creates a place to meet people where they are and then leads them onward to something better. We probably haven't arrived there yet, so we are still in the process of learning, developing, and growing, and that is the good side of what some call progressivism. But there must be conservatism as well; within progressivism the good that was already there is to be conserved and made better. It is not simply set aside. God has been developing people, individuals as well as groups, in this way throughout the passage of time. And eventually, in "the fullness of time" (Gal. 4:4), Christ came. A lot of people want to know why he didn't come as soon as the Israelites were out of Egypt or why he didn't just come directly to Abraham. And the answer is because God is working through the whole process of human history to develop a people who freely choose him, live for what is good, and trust in him alone.

IS SCRIPTURE PERFECT?

In the process of developing the covenant people God also gave them a book that is central to their identity. It is still central, although the people have changed, to the Christian church and to those identified as children of Abraham by faith. And just like the people of Israel, not everyone accepts their testimony, and their testimony is not perfect. Of course, the testimony of flawed humans wouldn't be perfect. But how about the Bible itself: Is it perfect?

My belief is that as God gave the scriptures, in their original form, they were absolutely perfect. But I don't know of any scholar, no matter how conservative, who would point to a particular version of the Bible in any language and say, "That one is inerrant." I believe the originals were inerrant, because I think that is the way God would have done it, but neither I nor any other living person has seen the originals, and frankly I'm rather glad we don't have them. Imagine what it would be like for some particular people to be in possession of them and what shenanigans would then follow!

We as a people need to confess that none of us have that perfect book. No one does. Why is this so? Is it possible that God did the best he could, but just couldn't hang on to it? Do you think that it is sort of like the story in *Raiders of the Lost Ark*? Have you ever thought about what it would be like if someone had the original manuscript that came from the hand of God?

The people of God are not perfect today either. Even your *pastor* is probably not perfect! And your initial response to that statement says a lot about where we are with this today, doesn't it? You see, when God approaches humanity, he sets things up in such a way that men and women have to seek God. I will give you some verses.

Let's just start with Deuteronomy 4—a prediction of what was going to happen to the Jewish people—these incredible people who still manage to exist:

> The Lord will scatter you among the peoples; only a few of you will be left among the nations where the Lord will lead you. There you will serve other gods made by human hands, objects of wood and stone that neither see, nor hear, nor eat, nor smell. From there you will seek the Lord your God, and you will find him if you search after him with all your heart and soul. (vv. 27–29)

You remember the famous statement in Jeremiah 50:4:

> In those days and at that time, says the Lord, the people of Israel shall come, they and the people of Judah together; they shall come weeping as they seek the Lord their God.

God's approach to humankind is one that allows us to hide, to not see him, but also to seek him (Deut. 4:29; 2 Chron. 15:15;

Jer. 29:13–14; Matt. 6:33; Acts 17:27). I encourage you to take your concordance and go through all of the statements in scripture about seeking the Lord.

Remember this: *To be a biblical Christian* is not to have high views about the Bible. *It is to seek and know and live the life that is depicted in the Bible.* The Jews of Jesus's time were people who prided themselves in their views and their knowledge of scripture. But in John 5:39–40 Jesus says to them:

> You search the scriptures because you think that in them you have eternal life; and it is they that testify on my behalf. Yet you refuse to come to me to have life.

Listen to these words from 2 Peter 3:15–16:

> So also our beloved brother Paul wrote to you according to the wisdom given him, speaking of this as he does in all his letters. There are some things in them hard to understand, which the ignorant and unstable twist to their own destruction, as they do the other scriptures.

One of the main things that people do with scriptures is to twist them. But notice that this is "to their own destruction." The Bible can kill you.

The Bible stands as an objective written witness in history to the word of God to us. It is a reliable record of God's revelation to you, whether you read it in *The Message* or in the original Hebrew or Greek. You can twist it and destroy your own soul. And if God set before you the perfect first version in which he himself saw to it that there were no mistakes, you could still kill yourself with it. And in fact, you would be more likely to, because you would probably make a temple where you could keep it safe and go worship it. And that is why we do not have it.

The scriptures are the best-attested record of the ancient world that we have. Normal standards of historical evidence authenticate them as reliable, historically and scientifically, so far as we can determine in every way. *But that will not bring you salvation.* When you come to the scriptures and say, "Beyond the sacred page I seek Thee, Lord. My spirit pants for Thee, O living Word!"[3] then the hand of God reaches out and touches the soul and brings you into that great purpose and reality that is God's redemptive act in human history. And any questions that arise about the nature of scripture or the people of God can be honestly dealt with. You can be open as you seek the truth and share in your fellowship the questions as well as the answers. God will bring us to the truth using our reason and, more than that, using the inspiration of the Holy Spirit to guide that reason.

It is possible to do more detailed studies on the reliability of scripture, although it is something that has been gone over very thoroughly, and there is a lot of good scholarship by people like F. F. Bruce[4] and others, who have written books that can really help people with the details. My feeling is that in apologetics, however, the real issues are not in the details. They are in the big issues: what the premises are, what the conclusions are, what the real questions are about, what doesn't make sense, and how to make sense of it.

Anyone who is really interested in seeing how this works out might want to look at *Classical Apologetics,* by R. C. Sproul, John Gerstner, and Arthur Lindsley.[5] Chapters 8 and 9 present an extremely good and convincing argument that the Bible, taken merely by the recognized standards of historiography, is demonstrably a reliable historical record, inspiration aside. If it is a reliable historical record, that means that it records the actual relationship of human beings to God, among other things, in the performance of miracles and so on and their testimony to scripture itself as the inspired word of God.

You may want to worry about that connection between miracle workers and inspiration. Jesus himself, in Matthew 7:21–23, talks about that. *Classical Apologetics* relates miracle workers to the testimony of inspiration, but I don't see that we *need* to make that link. I think we can simply proceed as follows: Scripture is a reliable, historical record of events in which scripture itself is testified to as the book of God. This is not the circular logic of people who say, "We know the Bible is true because it itself says it is." Instead, we say we know the Bible is true, because the standard canon of historiography authenticated it.

The issue of the reliability of the scriptures is a lot like the resurrection, in that most of those who *approach it in doubt* but remain merely *faithful to the details* find themselves believing, because the details contain such overwhelming evidence. If you approach it that way, you don't get caught in a circle; you have the testimony of a historically reliable record. It is not judged as historically reliable solely on the basis of its statements about itself. That historically reliable record, then, does make claims about itself, but since it is historically reliable, those statements are now equally reliable, and since those statements are reliable, we know they are inspired. Now, I don't think that argument is ever meant to stand by itself. I think it is meant to go hand in hand with the fact that anyone who approaches the Bible *for the purpose of finding God* will indeed find him and will be spoken to by God through the scriptures.

No one is going to be redeemed just by believing that the Bible is the inspired word of God. That alone won't save anybody. It certainly might have a good effect, but that is as far as you get. It is when the saving word of the gospel comes through the Bible or some other source and strikes faith in the heart, that we allow Christ into our lives and receive a new life from above, and we become full participants in the process toward God's goal in human history.

Chapter Six

THE PROBLEM OF PAIN AND EVIL

O that my words were written down!
O that they were inscribed in a book!
O that with an iron pen and with lead
they were engraved on a rock for ever!
For I know that my Redeemer lives,
and that at the last he will stand upon the earth;
and after my skin has been thus destroyed,
then in my flesh I shall see God,
whom I shall see on my side,
and my eyes shall behold, and not another.
My heart faints within me!

JOB 19:23–27

Some people regard the presence of pain in the world as a peculiarly deadly blow to the Christian faith. This is nothing to be wondered at. Most of us are inclined to think of the universe as anything but the kingdom of a benevolent and powerful God when we are having a bout with some painful physical or mental malady. It is easier to curse the world for being stupid and insensible to the priceless and admirable being we each know ourselves to be.

This "deadly" argument against Christianity runs in this fashion:

1. If Christianity is true, then God is both benevolent toward humankind and infinitely powerful.

2. If God is benevolent toward humankind and infinitely powerful, then he will see to it that we do not suffer.

3. God does not see to it that we do not suffer.

Therefore: Christianity is false, since God is either not benevolent or not powerful, to which the presence of suffering testifies.

A full appraisal of the issues involved in this argument would occupy several volumes of very small print. So I will go over only the key points necessary for us to evaluate the argument and be able to answer the questions it raises.[1]

A FORMALLY VALID ARGUMENT

I'm going to conduct a philosophy class with you for just a moment and tell you that the first thing we must ask ourselves in approaching any argument is whether it is formally valid. The argument presented above is formally valid. And by this I simply mean that, in the way this argument is stated, if we grant that the three premises are true, we must also grant that the conclusion is true. Failing to grant the conclusion after affirming the premises would be self-contradictory.[2]

Since the argument is formally valid, the only way the conclusion can be denied is to disprove one or all of the premises. But I should point out that even if this argument was not formally valid, we would still wish to call attention to the lack of truth in the premises. This is not because we are trying to get out of a tight spot, but because the premises are so manifestly untrue. The second premise is most objectionable, but we'll go through these in order and begin with the first one.

BENEVOLENT AND POWERFUL

According to the first premise, Christianity states that God is benevolent toward humankind and that he is infinitely powerful. Could we deny either of these two statements? Certainly we would not have the slightest desire to deny that God is benevolent toward humankind, for this is the very essence of the

Christian gospel. It is important here to point out that God's love is not a sentiment, but a well-reasoned devotion to the good or well-being of its objects. We have a terrible time understanding love, because we confuse it with desire. *Desire and love are two utterly different kinds of things.* Not only is desire not love; it is often *opposed* to love. Right action is the act of love, regardless of the desires of anyone involved.

In the second portion of this statement, that God is infinite in power, the situation is slightly different. We cannot confirm this with absolute certainty for the very simple reason that we cannot truly affirm something we cannot fully grasp. In my opinion, infinity is a concept that is best left to the mathematicians who have means for dealing with it. (Personally, I believe that God is infinite in power; I just don't know the formulas to prove it.)

This doesn't mean that we are going to say that God is *not* infinite in power. We must specify that God is always able to accomplish his will, that he is sufficient to the task of caring for his own business, and that a part of his business is taking care of human beings. Of course, this will immediately lead us to an examination of the second premise of the argument under discussion: if God is benevolent toward humankind and is able to carry out his will, then he will see to it that we do not suffer.

Now, this is the premise upon which the argument turns. If it is true, the argument that we are examining is not only valid, but will be admitted by many Christians as sound. If it is not true, then the argument is unsound: we state that we do not accept the premises and, therefore, need not accept the conclusion.

A good way to look at this is to ask what might possibly lead people to believe that a benevolent and all-powerful God would not allow humans to suffer. And when we ask this, we do not have to look far for an answer. If individuals were convinced that pain of any and all kinds was the worst possible thing that could happen to them, then they would believe, as a matter of course, that anyone who loved them—who was genuinely concerned for their welfare—and who also had the power to keep them from pain *would* actually keep them from pain. If they were not kept from pain by this powerful friend, they would think that they were dealing with someone who was either not powerful or not their friend, or both.

Notice the basis upon which this premise rests. It rests on the idea that the worst possible thing that can happen to a person is pain and that, as Aldous Huxley put in the mouth of one of his characters of *Brave New World,* "There isn't any need for a civilized man to bear anything that's seriously unpleasant."[3] Now, this is the heart of the argument. Can it seriously be maintained that pain serves no good end, that there is nothing to which pain is preferable, and that it is the ultimate of evils? These are three important questions that will be dealt with in reverse order.

SEPARATING PAIN FROM EVIL

First, is pain the ultimate of evils? Pain is not, in itself, evil at all. We just don't like it. But because I don't like boiled cabbage does not in the least mean that there is something wrong with cabbage. I don't like the looks of some people and I am sure they don't like mine, yet this does not mean there is anything morally wrong with either of us. Likewise, my dislike of pain does not in the least indicate that there is anything bad or wrong about it. It is a testimony only to the moral blindness of certain people that they equate what they dislike with what is bad or wrong. So pain or suffering is not in itself an evil, much less the ultimate evil.

Second, are there other things to which pain is preferable? Yes, there are, and I'll give you three good examples. People prefer living in pain to dying, even when they have no qualms about death itself—they simply value life under any condition as of higher worth than avoiding pain. Some people would take pain of any and all kinds upon themselves for any duration rather than betray certain convictions—political, moral, religious, or otherwise. And for those people who really know what friendship is, no cost in pain is too great to prevent the loss of a friend. If we knew what life totally devoid of any kind of pain was like, we would probably choose life with pain over life without it.

THE VALUE OF PAIN

This leads us to our third and final question. Could pain possibly serve any good end? Absolutely! First of all, it makes human life, as we know it, possible.[4] And, as strange as it may seem in the light of all the griping that is done, most people consider this life as we know it to be good. I am inclined to believe that Jeremy Bentham was quite right in the statement made at the opening of his *Introduction to the Principles of Morals and Legislation:*

Nature has placed mankind under the governance of two sovereign masters, pain and pleasure. It is for them alone to point out what we ought to do, as well as to determine what we shall do. On the one hand the standard of right and wrong, on the other the chain of causes and effects, are fastened to their throne. They govern us in all we do, in all we say, in all we think; every effort we can make to throw off our subjection will serve but to demonstrate and confirm it. In words a man may pretend to abjure their empire: but in reality he will remain subject to it all the while.[5]

Pleasure and pain are, in a word, the positive and negative poles between which flow the currents of human life. Detach one pole, and this life will cease. People who ask for a painless world don't truly know what they are asking for.

A second way in which pain serves a good is this. It is only in the heat of pain and suffering, both mental and physical, that real human character is forged. One does not develop courage without facing danger, patience without trials, wisdom without heart- and brain-racking puzzles, endurance without suffering, or temperance and honesty without temptations. These are the very things we treasure most about people. Ask yourself if you would be willing to be devoid of all these virtues. If your answer is no, then don't scorn the means of obtaining them. The gold of human character is dug from torturous mines, but its dung and dirt are quite easily come by. And it should come as no surprise to us that in our time—the time of the great flight from pain—such virtues as these are conspicuous only by their absence.

I'm not saying that we should go looking for pain, so that we can develop character. This is not at all necessary. All we need to do is make an honest and thorough effort to discover what is right and wrong, good and bad, and, when we are convinced on these points, then simply go out and face life for what it is worth. There will be plenty of opportunity to develop character. But you will never develop character by running from unpleasant situations, any more than you will develop your intellectual capacities by running away from study or tone up your "six-pack abs" by avoiding exercise.

REJECTION OF THE ARGUMENT

As you can see, my rejection of the argument that the presence of pain in our world means Christianity is false is based on the inaccuracy of the premise stating that, if a benevolent and powerful God did hold dominion over the proceedings of this world, he would not allow people to suffer. That this premise is false is obvious now that we understand that *God allows people to suffer precisely because he is benevolent.* It's for our best. I assume that God wishes to be able to write some epithet over the episode of human history other than, "And a good time was had by all." To hold that this second premise is true is to presuppose that God can only be good if he is a Jolly Good Fellow, running to satisfy our every whim and fancy and ease our every pain.

Upon careful consideration I am at a loss as to what kind of evidence might be brought forward in support of the view that human beings deserve paradisial treatment at the hands of God. Few people stop to ask themselves if they *deserve* to live in paradise. *They just want to.* And when they don't get what they want, they feel insulted. The fact is, it is people themselves who bring a great deal, if not the major part, of their suffering upon themselves. For instance, science now has at its disposal the knowledge with which to obliterate much of the serious physical suffering that prevails on the face of the earth. So why is this situation allowed to persist? Well, the simple truth is that human perversity in its various forms, refined and unrefined, will not allow the needed relief to get through. And yet people blame God for the effects of their own stubborn perversion.

IS GOD RESPONSIBLE
FOR ALL EVIL?

This leads us to a very important point. I have heard people attempt to place all the responsibility for what humankind does upon God by saying that God made human beings with the ability to do wrong, knowing that they would exercise that ability. God is, therefore, they say, responsible for all of the evil in the world.

If we use this principle to hold God responsible for human wrongdoing, it would be like holding parents responsible for the wrong their children do. The two cases are exactly the same on this point. If God is responsible for the wrongdoing of the humans he has given life to, then your father and mother are responsible for every lie you ever told and for everything you have ever done wrong. If your father and mother had any sense at all, they would have known that you would tell lies, in general make mistakes, and even intentionally do bad things on occasion. And yet your parents still made the decision to bring you into the world in spite of that knowledge. So the next time you fail a test, just tell the professor to give the "F" to your parents, for they gave you life, and with it the ability to fail tests.

It is notable that people who try to lay the responsibility for their behavior on God in this way cannot specify what sort of creature they would like to be after they give up their ability to do as they wish and forsake responsibility for their actions. They overlook the fact that by surrendering *responsibility* they surrender *freedom* and *the capacity for virtue* as well. The person who cannot be blameworthy cannot be praiseworthy either. As the old saying has it, these people throw out the baby with the bathwater.

Now, that's a rather silly way to talk about this particular criticism of God, but the questions surrounding the presence of evil in the world need to be taken very seriously. This is the single most urgent practical problem for Christian faith. We must be on guard not to talk about these issues *abstractly*— focusing only on God's omnipotence without regard to his moral purposes—or we'll find ourselves discussing the paradoxes of a God who "can do anything" and a universe of robots. We want to carefully process through these issues with a firm grip on reality and with the same method we used in addressing the presence of pain in the world. You will see that the argument begins in much the same fashion.

IF GOD IS GOOD

The classical argument from antiquity is, "If God *could* and is *good,* he *would*" prevent the death of this child (or whatever situation is at hand). This is the *only* argument of status against the existence of the Christian God. As with pain, many insist that if God were both all-good and all-powerful, he would not permit the evil things that do happen to occur at all. In the face of this problem, one is prone to think the deadliest of thoughts, namely, that God is not *good* or that he is not *able*. But if moral evil exists, aren't we forced to let go of one or the other?

To deal with this effectively, we need to understand the level of God's daily interaction in the realm of human affairs. Does *God* do everything there? Did *he* butter your toast this morning, drive your kids to school, write checks to pay your bills? No. Of course not! Human beings act too, and nature moves along in some degree on its own. All of this must be taken into consideration. So what we must look at is the question: Did God do well to create a world in which there is *free personality* and *natural law,* such that it includes the possibility of *a kingdom of God* as well as *the possibility of evil?*

Can we agree that many things ought not to be, without holding that the general framework that permits them to exist was a mistake on God's part? This returns us to our discussion of God's purpose within human history, which is to create for himself a living abode—a community of free, conscious, living beings. Could God have done this in a better way?

The world that contains the possibility of evil is the one that also contains the greatest possibility of good. And the question of why God allows evil to happen has to be put against the question of what a world where evil could not happen would be like. It's by working on those questions that people can come to some resolution in their minds about the reality of evil and what it means.

"IN A PERFECT WORLD"

Let's consider another criticism of the way God has made humankind and the world. How do we respond to the proposal that God is blameworthy not for an act of commission, but for an act of omission—not for making humankind in a way that allows them to do wrong, but for not making humankind wholly good and placing them in a wholly good environment where no wrong could be done?

When people vilify God for failing to make a wholly good world inhabited by wholly good people, I fear that they are not always concerned with moral goodness. Many times they only mean that God should have made a world in which *they* would always get what they want and one that would be inhabited by people of the sort *they* like. I suspect that all of the complaints we hear about the way the world runs are only so many variations on a theme spelled out so exquisitely in the *Rubáiyát* of Omar Khayyám:

> *Ah Love! could you and I with Him conspire*
> *To grasp this sorry Scheme of Things entire,*
> *Would not we shatter it to bits—and then*
> *Re-mould it nearer to the Heart's Desire!*[6]

We humans never get what we want, and, oh, we want it so badly! We want it badly enough to conclude without hesitation that God should have designed this world with our specific needs in mind.

WHY WON'T GOD
DO IT *MY* WAY?

The people who draw the conclusion that God should have made a wholly good world with wholly good people should stop to consider three things. First, we do not have any evidence to show us that the "good" world we are blaming God for not creating would suit us any better than this one. It may well be only another case of the greener grass on the other side of the fence. And the fact that many people believe that this life is good suggests that, instead of there being something wrong with this world, the real trouble lies within the people who are in such a hurry to get away from it.

Second, why should God be under more of an obligation to suit the taste of the objectors to this world and provide them with a world that they like than to suit the taste of the great many people who actually find life as it is to be good? If God were going to suit everybody, he would simply have to make separate and distinct worlds, each containing a single person. But then no one would like this, because everyone would be lonely.

Third, the proposition that God is obligated to suit personal taste is far from self-evident. People who argue that God is obligated to create such and such kind of world are really only saying, "God must do what I want him to do, or he is a bad, bad boy. I'll take my marbles and go home."

THERE IS NO "GOOD"
WITHOUT "EVIL"

If God had created a wholly "good" environment and placed wholly "good" people in it, these people would not be able to refer to themselves or their world as *good,* to their acts as *right,* or to their life as *pleasant.* These are all correlative concepts that lose their meaning in the absence of their opposites. Such a world would not be good to the people who were in it and the people themselves would not be good. Or, more correctly, it would be senseless to *say* they were good, since the concept "good" has application only in a world where good has to live side by side with evil. In such a world, there would be no moral life at all, and consequently no *human* beings as we understand humanity to be. To ask to live in such a world, then, is the same as asking to not be human.

CHARACTER DEVELOPMENT

If you think deeply about it, you'll understand the great value of an environment that provides human beings with choice and the possibility of developing good character or poor character. When we tell children to "make good choices," are we just hoping they will manage to stay out of trouble for the day, or that the "good choices" will become habits and the children will grow into people who naturally do the right thing? *A world that permits the development of moral character*—one that makes it possible for persons to become the immeasurably precious and even glorious beings that they sometimes do become—*is of much greater value than any world that does not.*

When we look at something as terrible as a terrorist attack, we might be inclined to say we'd be better off in a world that just has vegetables and minerals. But if you think about it a bit, you'll realize that nearly everything in your life that is of value would be gone. There wouldn't be any evil, but there also wouldn't be any good. It's because of the great value of what is good in human life that a world that allows for evil, but also responsibility for good, is much more valuable and desirable— even with the pain—than a world that has only minerals and vegetables, or nothing at all.

If personality and character are not regarded as having a very great value, it would clearly be wrong of God to permit the actual suffering and wrongdoing that occurs in order to procure it. *But the moral development of personality is possible only in a world of genuine freedom.* If you take this down to the level of raising children, and you suggest that it might be better if we could prevent them from doing anything that is harmful, you realize that if you do that, you will destroy their lives. *They* have to choose, *they* have to learn, and *they* have to grow.

To nurture moral perfection, horrendous moral crimes must be permitted by God—though he himself never approves of, actualizes, or requires them. Nurturing moral perfection (within a suitable world) and not allowing wrongdoing is impossible. If children are never permitted to do wrong, they will never become capable of developing a nature or character that resolutely chooses the good. *Good persons must live in a world where doing evil is a readily available option.* Producing people with character without giving them choice is impossible, because the capacity to choose is a part of character.

The character of an individual develops through *action,* modified and reflected upon in its consequences and repeated over time. The *context* of this action for the novice or child has a character that is predefined by its social climate and customs. This culture-character also develops and evolves, but *only* through historical processes. So you see how human personality rests on past generations for its initial character. This is each person's genetic and cultural starting point. Its development also is historical in the *larger* sense, in which we speak of *world* and *human* history.

THE IMPORTANCE OF ORDER

Some may ask if it is possible for God to have created the world with *less* evil. If he had just prevented Hitler, would that have made this a better world? The image here is one in which God sits up there with a great big flyswatter, and whenever he sees something evil about to happen, he hits it. But what you get out of that is a world in which there is no order, and no law. You can't count on what's going to happen, because you don't know when God is going to step in and swat something.

The nature of human action and interaction requires a reign of law or orderliness. This predictable order makes it possible to set goals, plan their realization, learn from one's mistakes, and above all interact with other persons to form a community. Even a family (perhaps especially a family) cannot properly form without a framework of established and commonly known rules and expectations. The free, conscious engagement of individual personality with its surroundings is required. But if you can't count on consistent responses to your actions, it becomes impossible to learn what actions are appropriate. How would you feel if you stepped on the accelerator and the car came to a screeching halt, or if you poured water on a fire and the flames flared up as if you had poured gasoline on them? How do you know what you are supposed to do to achieve the desired result in each situation? You would become paralyzed by fear of the unknown consequences of each possible action.

A world with laws of nature, social mores, and a regular sequence of activity, in which you have the ability to "make good choices" or not with full awareness of the consequences, is the only environment that will give individual human beings the opportunity to develop a personality and character of their own—whether to their glory or their detriment. If you are going to have moral agents in community, you must have something very like our world.

DILEMMA DISSOLVED

So the presence of moral evil in the world does not mean that God is lacking in goodness or power. The classical dilemma is dissolved by setting existing evil in the context of the good that God achieves in permitting (but not producing) moral evil. This conclusion permits us to see the suffering of individuals, ourselves or others, in the larger world of a great and good

God, who has all eternity and resources beyond our wildest imagination to ensure that the life of every individual who suffers, in whatever way, is ultimately one that even that individual will receive with boundless gratitude.

THE CHRISTIAN RESPONSE

How then do we reply to the objections that the creator and sustainer of a world in which there is war, deformity, suicide, depression, earthquakes, famine, pestilence, and cancer cannot be a *good* God, able to assist those who trust him and those who must depend upon his care?

First, we agree that many things that happen, *when considered by themselves,* are not good. They are indeed tragic. We must never deny this. It's important not to give a cavalier or simple answer to those who have suffered. You have to accept the full reality of suffering and not try to explain it away. Let those who suffer tell you their story and really listen to them. Where was God? God is always where the suffering is. Those who are there and turn to him will find him.

Imagine yourself talking to someone whose loved one was on the top floor of the World Trade Center when it was collapsing. You could never say anything to diminish the pain they actually feel or explain it away. But you can say that there is something beyond the pain. Those who look to God and call upon him can be sure that good will triumph in their lives.

Second, we agree that God is not the *agent* behind these things. God doesn't *do* evil. He knows better. It's the same reason I don't stick a pen in my eye. It's because I know better.

God designed a world where people have space to choose their own actions, starting at the very beginning with Adam and Eve, and there is an enemy in the picture taking advantage of this. On the larger scale, we all know this.

The book of Job is important here. It helps us understand we're in a battle. After reading Job, you might think it would be a good idea not to call the Devil's attention to yourself by being too good, but testing will still come. God does not torture or send suffering upon his people. Sometimes he allows them to experience suffering, because they've walked away from him, but suffering doesn't always occur for that reason. It occurs because there is an enemy who wishes to make you doubt God. In the overall picture, that is the meaning of the book of Job. In the middle of all his pain and losses, Job says, "Though he slay me, yet will I trust in him" (13:15, KJV). Your trust in God is what matters.

Now, no matter what the difficulties are, and sometimes they're extremely hard to bear, we do not want to doubt God. We want to cling to God. If we think, "God is testing me," we're apt not to focus on him. Let me assure you that God does not need to test you to find out about you. I have to test my students to find out about them, but God doesn't have that problem. He already knows. So understand that testing comes, but it's not God's work to test by causing suffering. He knows who we are, and he knows what we can bear. When trouble does come, the important thing is to understand that God is against it.

Third, we point out that the creation of a world with a general order in which pain and evil are possible is good, beyond any comparison possible to us. And it is the *greatest conceivable good,* giving humanity the opportunity to develop into creatures of the highest value. C. S. Lewis wrote:

It is a serious thing to live in a society of possible gods and goddesses, to remember that the dullest, most uninteresting person you talk to may one day be a creature which, if you saw it now, you would be strongly tempted to worship, or else a horror and a corruption such as you now meet, if at all, only in a nightmare. All day long we are, in some degree, helping each other to one or the other of these destinations. . . . There are no ordinary people. You have never talked to a mere mortal. Nations, cultures, arts, civilizations—these are mortal, and their life is to ours as the life of a gnat. But it is immortals whom we joke with, work with, marry, snub, and exploit—immortal horrors or everlasting splendors. . . . Next to the holy sacrament itself, your neighbor is the holiest object presented to your senses.[7]

Fourth, we maintain that "earth has no sorrow that heaven cannot heal."[8] The battle is not over yet, and God *is* going to win. To single out a specific sorrow as evil forever is to question the Christian view of God and our eternal destiny in God's great universe. Romans 8:28 tells us: "All things work together for good for those who love God, who are called according to his purpose." If we have committed our lives to God, he will restore us in our life here on earth, as he promised Israel in Joel 2:25–27:

> I will repay you for the years
> that the swarming locust has eaten,
> the hopper, the destroyer, and the cutter,
> my great army, which I sent against you.
> You shall eat in plenty and be satisfied,
> and praise the name of the Lord your God,
> who has dealt wondrously with you.

And my people shall never again be put to shame.
You shall know that I am in the midst of Israel,
and that I, the Lord, am your God and there is no other.
And my people shall never again be put to shame.

God will also redeem every aspect of our lives in the hereafter. The claim that this present suffering is beyond redemption can only be true if we know that a God of Christian dimensions does not exist. We hold to the promise given in Revelation 21:3–4:

See, the home of God is among mortals.
He will dwell with them;
they will be his peoples,
and God himself will be with them;
He will wipe every tear from their eyes.
Death will be no more;
mourning and crying and pain will be no more,
for the first things have passed away.

The Christian faith is committed to a picture of God and the world that makes every event ultimately redeemable, and therefore permissible, by a personal God who is both willing and able to nurture into being a creation that cannot be improved upon. It does not hold that every event is good in itself. Bad things, even horrendous moral evils, do come to pass. But in the vision of Jesus Christ communicated to his people, all human beings—and yes, even the sparrows and the lilies—are effectively cared for. Every person is invited to say in faith and obedience, "The Lord is my shepherd, I shall not want."

If all the individual has is "this" life, then clearly evil, pain, and frustration are not redeemed. But seen in the context of God's world as a whole, seen as but a part of a life that never ends and endlessly becomes more and more glorious, there is no evil individuals may suffer that can prevent them from finding life to be good and God to be good. Theirs is the perspective of the apostle Paul, who speaks of great suffering as "this slight momentary affliction [that] is preparing us for an eternal weight of glory beyond all measure, because we look not at what can be seen but at what cannot be seen; for what can be seen is temporary, but what cannot be seen is eternal" (2 Cor. 4:17–18).

We get a little taste of that in this life. When we move into the future and the future is good, the past, which was unbearable when we went through it, now takes on a different quality because it's a part of the larger whole. It's the greatness and goodness of God that matters. Even David Hume, who is well known for his skepticism, says, "If your God is big enough, there is no problem of evil" (my paraphrase).⁹ That's the key. Jesus affirms that in our lives, and we can go on from that and experience the goodness of God as we face each new day.

The child who dies during a famine is ushered immediately into the full world of God in which he or she finds existence good and prospects incomprehensibly grand. There God is seen, as he now surely is not seen, to be good and great without limit, and every individual received into his presence enjoys the everlasting sufficiency of his goodness and greatness. There is no tragedy for those who rely on this God.

HUMAN RESPONSIBILITY

I am of the considered opinion that there is no desirable alternative to a life that includes a certain amount of pain, struggle, disappointment, and suffering in general for human beings. But I am not trying to say, in the words of the good Pangloss, a character in Voltaire's *Candide* (1759): "All is for the best in the best of all possible worlds." Far from it! However, I am willing to say that it *could be* the best of all possible worlds for human life, were it not for human perverseness and stupidity.

We as human beings have a long way to go. But no good will come of either blaming God for our ills or sitting around waiting for God to do what we ought to have the sense and ambition enough to accomplish for ourselves. God has put the natural abilities and means at our disposal with which to make this world a decent and pleasant place to live. This is precisely the reason why he will hold us responsible for failing at the task. And all those who charge God with the evil of this world lay themselves open to the charge of insincerity unless they are doing all within their power to dispel the evil of this world.

If, for example, people foolishly expend their economic resources, they only prove themselves to be hypocrites when they fault God for allowing human beings to go hungry. And contrary to much current opinion, one need not profess any religion whatsoever to be a hypocrite. If those who reproach God for the pain and evil in this world are sincere, why don't they start where they are (for we need not look far for pain and evil) and do something about it? Of course, some do. Thankfully, *some* do.

THE OTHER PROBLEM OF EVIL

This brings us to the "other" problem of evil: how to get rid of it. If I am truly concerned about moral evil in the world, I should at least worry as much about my responsibility for it as about God's. By personally ceasing to do evil, I can make a significant impact on the moral evil in my world. By trusting the goodness and greatness of God, I can turn loose of the chain that drags me into moral evil—the chain of self-deification, which puts me in the position of being the only one I trust to take care of me. Nearly all evildoing occurs under the guise of "necessity." I wouldn't lie, cheat, steal, or harm others, if it weren't necessary to secure *my* aims—which of course *I* must bring about.

A primary form of evil is the desire to harm people, whether it's in a bully in the schoolyard or a national leader like Hitler or Mussolini. Its root cause is anger. Anger comes from disappointment of one's desires. The foundation of this whole discussion is the fundamental fact that people want things they don't get, so they become angry and are ready to hurt other people.

In the Sermon on the Mount, Jesus starts his discussion of life with a picture of the kingdom of God and the blessed life within that. And then he turns to street level and begins to look at where harm comes from in individual lives. The first thing he puts his finger on is anger and contempt (Matt. 5:21–26).[10] If you could pull anger and contempt out of the world, you wouldn't have an attack on the Twin Towers, or a Holocaust, or an Inquisition. Without anger and contempt, there simply isn't the motivation to hurt people.

It's important to remember this as we look at evil in the world and ask, "What am I going to do about it?" We each have to start with ourselves and our range of influence. We need to help others come to grips with the place of anger and desire in their lives. Anger comes from crossing someone's will—interfering with someone's desires. The general path of changing this, of getting rid of anger and contempt and keeping desire under control,[11] is to surrender our will to God. That is to say, we have to turn our future, our present, and everything in our lives over to God's care. This is the answer to the problem of evil. Even for those who have to go through cancer, losing loved ones, war, whatever it may be—the answer is surrender to the will of God.

If I rely upon God, I can relinquish the realization of my aims to him. I can stop doing what I and everyone else know to be wrong, and I can calmly cease cooperation with immoral behavior occurring around me. I also can stand against the evils in my world unconcerned about what is going to happen to me if I do. We need not try to be perfect. We can concentrate on just doing a lot better. That is the surest way of vastly improving the world we live in.

JESUS AS OUR MODEL

The best way of taking this stand against evil is by simply relying on Jesus Christ to guide and help us. In him we can find the mold or image in which we may be remade. The whole of the Christian message may be summed up as the call to be conformed to this image (see Romans 8:29). The claim of Christ on the lives of men and women consists simply in this: that he is what they ought to be. He is the unique embodiment of all those traits of character that we call virtues. And he adds this yet above all: that he exemplifies living, direct communion with God. *Christianity understood as the discipline of Christ is the true humanism.* Christ is the human image, and because he is this, he is also the express image of God's personality. One can also state it the other way and say that because Christ is the express image of God's personality, he is the human image. The outstanding characteristics of this image, at once human and divine, are given by Paul in his letter to the Galatians as "love, joy, peace, patience, kindness, generosity, faithfulness, gentleness, and self-control" (5:22–23).

To surrender authority over our lives to Christ means, among other things, to acknowledge him as the ideal of human life, as the one who embodies every virtue and goodness that you and I ought to embody. But to recognize him as this is also to recognize him as one who is uniquely the Son of God, for he preeminently exemplifies that godlikeness that constitutes the family resemblance connecting all of God's children.

The difference between Christ and others in the family of God lies in the fact that he never turns his will against the will of the Father. The others do and, in so doing, lose the family resemblance and allow a place for evil. We all *can* do what is right, but for the most part we don't want to. We would much prefer to do what is easy or pleasant. We would, in short, rather do what *we* want than what God wants or what the moral law demands. To go contrary to the will of the Father is to reject his lordship and leave his family. But any who do so can reenter the family of God by placing themselves at God's disposal with the simple request that God restore the *imago Dei*, the image of God, which they have stricken from themselves by their own obstinate willfulness and pride.

THE HOUND OF HEAVEN

I could do no better in summing up all that I have tried to say here than to quote a passage from the writings of Francis Thompson, an English poet of over a century ago who lived a life of disease and personal sorrow. This quotation, which comes at the close of his poem entitled "The Hound of Heaven,"[12] is in the form of a dialogue between God and the poet, whom God has pursued through life. God speaks:

> *And human love needs human meriting:*
> *How hast thou merited—*
> *Of all man's clotted clay the dingiest clot?*
> *Alack, thou knowest not*
> *How little worthy of any love thou art!*
> *Whom wilt thou find to love ignoble thee*
> *Save Me, save only Me?*
> *All which I took from thee I did but take,*
> *Not for thy harms,*
> *But just that thou might'st seek it in My arms.*
> *All which thy child's mistake*
> *Fancies as lost, I have stored for thee at home:*
> *Rise, clasp My hand, and come!*

Then says the poet, referring to the feet that have followed him through life:

> *Halts by me that footfall:*
> *Is my gloom, after all,*
> *Shade of His hand, outstretched caressingly?*

God answers:

> *Ah, fondest, blindest, weakest,*
> *I am He Whom thou seekest!*
> *Thou drawest love from thee, who drawest Me.*

There is no room or use for discouragement in this life, much less for bitterness, if we will only look discerningly at ourselves and place our hope in the love of God manifested in the person of Christ for all people to share.

Chapter Seven

LIVING AND
ACTING WITH GOD

The Lord is my shepherd, I shall not want.
He makes me lie down in green pastures;
he leads me beside still waters; he restores my soul.
He leads me in right paths for his name's sake.

Even though I walk through the darkest valley, I fear no evil;
for you are with me; your rod and your staff—they comfort me.

You prepare a table before me in the presence of my enemies;
you anoint my head with oil; my cup overflows.
Surely goodness and mercy shall follow me all the days of my life,
and I shall dwell in the house of the Lord my whole life long.

PSALM 23

The ultimate apologetic is the life of the individual who is living out of the resources of the kingdom of God. To have a nice set of abstract ideas and arguments can be very important for us, but we need to be people who are actually accomplishing things in the kingdom of the heavens through our prayers and our words. We live in a personal relationship with God, and we need to discuss what that means.

There are three points to address. One has to do with the nature of reality. Is reality personal? That is the cultural question. Do you ever lie in bed at night and wonder about this little ball of earth twirling around out here in this endless space? You can sometimes feel greatly intimidated by looking at physical reality. You can be victimized if you don't understand that that reality reasonably and logically implies that there is an infinite personal being that made it and holds it together.

Now, this is crucial to our faith, but many people seek to share their faith by going directly to a topic like the resurrection of Christ. But those already committed to the idea of something coming out of nothing and order coming out of chaos won't even think twice about the idea that someone came back from the dead. It's just another strange thing in a strange universe.

I have friends and acquaintances who have made a business out of going to college campuses to debate Christians in organizations like Campus Crusade and InterVarsity. I've heard them say, "It would be very strange, but if I stood there and watched Jesus Christ coming out of the tomb, coming back to life and walking around, it wouldn't imply that a God existed." You have to remember, in a universe that is not already clearly in the hands of God, there is no background for interpreting those events. Jesus said, "Believe in God, believe also in me" (John 14:1). There's an order of events in that statement.

It is the existence of "the Great I Am" that is testified to by nature. It is the redemptive process of history that lays the foundation for Jesus to come. Why didn't Jesus come instead of Cain? Cain was the first one born, and after all God did say that Eve's offspring would strike the serpent's head (Gen. 3:15). So why wasn't Jesus born right away? You have to understand that God is a person and approaches people redemptively as a person. If you don't understand that, then you can't get into these other points, and especially the ones I am about to cover.

Remember that we must use an orderly process and lay appropriate groundwork as we proceed in apologetics. So *after* we talk about redemptive history with a covenant people and a book, we talk about an incarnation if we have time, and *then* a resurrection.

After all of that, we come to our second point and the heart of the matter. When people ask, "Why are you hopeful in the midst of this world, with all of the suffering and evil that goes on and all of the things that are happening to you?" they don't want to hear merely about a great God. They don't want to hear merely about redemptive history, an infallible book, or a covenant people who are a constant testimony to the real hand of God in history. They want to know what's happening to *you,* what's going on in *your* life. You are saying, "He is my fortress, he is my deliverer." So they're going to want to know when the last time he delivered you was. What does deliverance mean? How does this really work? Sharing the good news is often about sharing the personal good news of your life in Christ and not the abstract and generalized good news. They want to hear about your personal relationship to this personal God, who is the foundation of all of reality.

When we move into apologetics beyond the first level, beyond the issue of God's existence and basic nature, our work becomes less a matter of proof (though that is still absolutely crucial at certain points) and more a matter of making sense of the elements of Christian faith. We need to be living proof of the reality of life as we know it to be. The word came in times past to people who received it as a real part of their life and spirit. Redemptive history, scripture, and the life of Jesus here on this earth were things that happened to real people.

Which brings us to our third point: Did all of that communication from God stop when the Bible closed? Is that the last thing that has been heard from God? Is *that* a personal relationship? Some people talk as if their personal relationship to God were simply a matter of a credit arrangement having been made for them, so that when they die all of their charges will be written off. Is *that* a personal relationship?

All of the things we see in the Bible are there to teach us what is real and present to us today. When we read about God invading history in the lives of individuals, we are dealing with a reality that is continuing, and unless it continues, there really is nothing that you can call a personal relationship to God. If all there is to Christianity is getting the right belief and going to heaven when you die, what is the role of human existence from here on? Yes, it is certainly to preach the gospel and to invite others to receive the grace of God in salvation, but is that all there is to it? Or are we to live *now* in union with God in his kingdom?

The presupposition of all of the New Testament teachings is that we will have a personal walk with God, and that will be a matter of real events that occur in our lives as we live and work *with him,* where we are, as his children. And that is what, finally, will be the only satisfactory answer to our friend who asks, "What is going on in your life?" The answer *has* to be, "I will tell you and I will show you how it works in my life, and you can have it too. You really can know what it is like to deal with God and for God to deal with you in the daily moments of your existence." God creates and sustains personal relationships with individuals by his individual word to them, within the confines of biblical teachings. *His kingdom works by words!*

One of the crucial things that must be discussed in the helping ministry of apologetics is the ministry of dealing with doubt and removing it by clarifications as directed by the Holy Spirit: God's speaking to us.

DOES GOD SPEAK TO US?

One of the most tremendously important topics in apologetics is the issue of God's speaking to us. Can you imagine what a personal relationship would be like with someone who never spoke to you? A lot of people believe that God does not speak to individuals, but they go to church and sing:

> *He walks with me and he talks with me,*
> *and he tells me I am his own,*
> *and the joy we share as we tarry there,*
> *none other has ever known.*[1]

We sing many songs without attaching any real meaning to the words, and say, "Well, it's just music."

Many people are never comfortable with the idea that God would speak to them. And since God is not going to run over them or tap them on the shoulder when a message is coming through, very often they will testify that, indeed, God has never spoken to them.

HEARING GOD SPEAK

I believe the single most important thing I have to do is to encourage people to believe that God *will* speak to them and that they can come to understand and recognize his voice. There are many beautiful stories in the Bible about this. Read the story in Genesis 24, about Abraham's sending his eldest servant back to his relatives to find a wife for his son Isaac. It's an important task, and the servant is clearly worried about it; he asks Abraham what to do if he can't get a woman to come back with him. Abraham tells him that the Lord will "send his angel before" him (v. 7). The man doesn't believe a word of it. Yet when he gets there, he asks the "God of [his] master Abraham" (v. 12) for success in his mission, and "before he had finished speaking, there was Rebekah . . ." (v. 15). It's a wonderful story about the process through which the servant learns about coming to God for guidance.

God speaks constantly to people, but most of them don't know what's happening. They are like the prophet Samuel, who as a child was staying with the priest Eli. The Lord came to Samuel's bed and called to him, "Samuel! Samuel!" Thinking it must be Eli, Samuel got up and went to Eli, who said he hadn't called him and sent him back to bed. This happened a few more times until finally Eli realized what was happening. In that beautiful story in 1 Samuel 3, Eli told Samuel that if he was called again, he was to say, "Speak, Lord, for your servant is listening" (v. 9). There are all kinds of explanations for why people do not hear the voice of God, or why they hear it, but don't know what it is. But you must learn how God speaks; not doing so will constantly undermine your confidence in your personal relationship to him.

However, often you will hear people testifying to the fact that God did speak with them. This morning in church a lady spoke about being married to a person who wasn't a Christian. She was not a Christian either when they married, but she later converted. At a certain point she was considering leaving her husband because of problems in their marriage. As she sat one day, she said, God spoke to her, telling her exactly why she should stay in the marriage. That is a personal relationship with God. If you have your mind set that it is impossible for God to speak to you individually, that is your faith. And as it is your faith, at least as far as your experience is concerned, that is probably the way it is going to be for you.

Now, sometimes God does strange things to get people's attention, but the fundamental way God speaks to us is by causing thoughts in our mind that we come to learn have a characteristic quality, content, and spirit about them. Think about how we speak to each other. I speak to you by making noises, and little sound waves go into your ears and bounce around on your eardrums in a pattern that your brain converts into language. The ultimate result of that act is that you have a thought. I speak to you by causing thoughts in your mind. Once you have gotten that idea clear, then it can be pretty simple to see that God has many ways of causing thoughts in our mind. (That's if you have established any basis at all for the idea that there *is* a God, that he made us, that there is a purpose in human history, and so on.)

You will clearly see God speaking in many ways as you study the scriptures. In Numbers 11 and Exodus 33 we see that God speaks to Moses as one speaks to a friend, face-to-face. In Jeremiah, you will see dreams contrasted with the word of the Lord: "Let the prophet who has a dream tell the dream, but let the one who has my word speak my word faithfully. . . . Is not my word like fire, says the Lord, and like a hammer that breaks a rock in pieces?" (23:28–29). There's no suggestion that it is audible. Jesus himself seemed to have been one who directly heard God's voice. Later on people needed things to get their attention, like Saul on the road to Damascus and others in the book of Acts. I don't think we should rule out any options, but we should understand that God's preferred mode is to address willing hearers by the thoughts that are given to their minds, the "still small voice" of 1 Kings 19:12 (KJV).

LEARNING THE MASTER'S VOICE

We learn voices by experience. We are at least as smart as sheep. They learn to identify the voices of their masters by experience. That is one of the images the scriptures use over and over to emphasize the learning of the voice. In time, you learn the difference in the spirit, the tone, and the content of the thoughts that come to mind. You can get pretty good at recognizing whether a thought has come to you from God. For one thing, God will never nag or whine at you. By contrast, I have found that there is always a quality of nervousness, of tinniness, about one's own thoughts.

If you wish to know the voice of God as it comes to you individually, simply allow yourself to trust God to lead you into that. Ask God to speak to you and then wait attentively. He will probably speak to you clearly. But you have to understand and believe that this is even possible. Otherwise your faith will not rise to it, and you will not have the opportunity to learn. The reason I emphasize this here is because, when your friend asks about your relationship with God and the reason for your hope, you don't want to be in the position of saying, "Well, he never speaks to *me,* but he speaks to lots of other people."

A PERSONAL EXAMPLE

Many people ask me to give examples of times I have clearly heard God communicate with me. I will briefly give you one that will stick with you. I have a son who was helping me with some computer work for a book many years ago. We had just made plans for the next part of the project, and as I walked into the next room, there came to me, in the way that I have learned to recognize, the thought, "He will never live to finish it." I am not going to try to prove to you that it was God; I am just telling you what I experienced.

I believe prayer makes a difference. I believe that is why we pray. If you don't believe that you change God's mind when you pray, you won't pray. That is the only reason for it. So I went to prayer, and after a while I received assurance that my son would not die.

The following Sunday, we received a call from the highway patrol saying that our son had been in an automobile accident, and he was in very serious condition. He had been taken to intensive care at UCLA Medical Center. So I continued in prayer as we made our way to the hospital. I must tell you that he, as well as everyone else around, was quite convinced that a series of unusual things occurred throughout this incident. For example, a nurse and a doctor were immediately behind him at the scene of the accident, and they were able to supervise his care from the beginning. There were other things like that. He recovered, and I know that this has made a great difference for him spiritually.

I give such a dramatic example, because I think you will remember that. But the point is that I have learned the quality of what comes to me from God. One of the things I began to realize over time is that for many years God spoke to me and told me to do things, and I didn't know it was him. I just thought it was me thinking.

OBJECTIONS TO HEARING FROM GOD

Many kinds of objections have been raised about the idea of God speaking to us. For example, many people feel that this is a threat to the authority of the scriptures. No, it is a threat to the authority of the scriptures to teach and to act as if God does *not* speak to individuals, because it is the clear teaching of the scriptures that he *does* speak. Read John 14. Read the book of Acts. You will see that he does. Scripture stands as an objective historical measurement of what God will say. It's important to remember that no communication that God ever gives to anyone will ever conflict with scripture, but he also needs to say a lot of things to you that aren't in scripture.

For example, as far as I know, there is no place in scripture that says anything at all about the church you are currently attending. Yet I trust that your leaders and fellow church members are receptive to the possibility that God might convey his will to your church about specific decisions you are making. On the other hand, one of the reasons we get into such trouble with this is because we are constantly looking to God to help us make decisions. We are nervous, we want to make the right decision, and we say, "Oh, Lord, tell me what to do."

But we mustn't get neurotic about this; God's guidance to us in his word is not designed to replace our commitment to him in faith. And we often must step out in our decisions, trusting God without a specific word from him.

We also need to understand that if God wants us to know something, he will tell us. He doesn't play games. I have seen people get into discussions about guidance, and before they know it, they are saying things that are blasphemous, because they are suggesting that God can't quite get the information to us. He would like to, but he just can't. Or they get in a bind about infallibility: "Well, if God spoke to me that would make *me* infallible." You know, he spoke to a lot of people in the scriptures and, with one exception, none of them were infallible.

The idea that God might speak directly to individuals worried many of the people in biblical times, like the Sadducees, who didn't believe in angels, resurrection, or that God talked to anybody after he got done talking with Moses! They were nervous about the whole idea. (That's why they were sad, you see.)

TESTING WHAT WE HEAR

We do have to be concerned about people who say "God told them" to do something crazy. We should also be concerned with people understanding that scripture is the canon. No prophecy is of private interpretation, and I never believe anyone who makes a big deal that God told them something, unless God told somebody else the same thing. I practice that in my family. I will never say, "Jane, we are going to do this because God told me." I will ask her, "What did God tell you?"

THE THREE LIGHTS

One way of testing what you hear is to use what Frederick B. Meyer's book *The Secret of Guidance* describes as the "three lights": circumstances, impressions of the Spirit, and passages from the Bible. Rick Warren adds a fourth: "the godly wisdom of Christian counsel." Meyer says:

> God's impressions within and his word without are always corroborated by His providence around, and we should quietly wait until these three focus into one point. . . . If you do not know what you ought to do, stand still until you do. And when the time comes for action, circumstances, like glowworms, will sparkle along your path. You will become so sure that you are right, when God's three witnesses concur, that you could not be surer though an angel beckoned you on.[2]

Test what you hear and what those around you say they are hearing. In my book *Hearing God,* you will find an extensive discussion on testing what you hear,[3] but I'll just say briefly that the ultimate test in verifying what you may be hearing is that it is in agreement with the scriptures. Of course, if you are unwilling to do what scripture already teaches, there is not much point in saying, "Lord, tell me more." So comparison to scripture is the ultimate test of the content of the message, but it is also the ultimate test of our spirit—if we are following what we find in scripture to begin with.

THE REALITY OF A PERSONAL RELATIONSHIP WITH GOD

Although hearing a message from God is an area we must guard carefully, we cannot allow that to undercut the reality of a personal God speaking intimately with individuals. This is what gives people hope. This is what enables them to face all of the trials and even death itself in complete confidence that they are in the hands of a God who will never turn them loose. "And this is eternal life, that they may know you, the only true God, and Jesus Christ whom you have sent" (John 17:3). And that knowledge is a personal one.

If we are going to have a personal relationship with God, we are going to have to come to terms with the concerns expressed by those who have not experienced what we are talking about. And as we approach this matter, we have to recognize that in relationship to those who have not yet come to faith, *apologetics must move away from the level of argument toward the realm of real-life experience.* So the primary work of a Christian apologetic at this point is to help Christians overcome their confusion or doubt about their daily personal interaction with God.

This is difficult work, because it puts each of us on the line. I mean, you would feel that I should have something personal to do with God in my role as a minister, wouldn't you? And the same would be true for any ministers, right? Don't you feel that we ought to occasionally talk to God? And perhaps, after the discussion above, that he would occasionally talk to us? Clearly, you would expect a minister to have some direct, personal dealings with God. Most Christians would also believe that what is true of the ministry should be true of everyone among the redeemed. Isn't that right? We are talking about what our religious life really consists of. And I want to simply say that it consists of God's speaking to us in his word as well as personally, our speaking to God, and then finally our speaking *with* God. In our conversations of prayerful love with God, we must move beyond giving God a list of wants, needs, and desires and move into deeper conversations with God about what we are doing together in his world.

OUR INTERACTION WITH GOD

As we approach the concept of speaking in partnership *with* God, we have to recall that we live in a personal universe. Everything around us is held together by personal acts of God. For example, Jesus spoke to the waves of the sea. Now, if you don't understand that the waves of the sea are held together in the personal word of God, you might be puzzled about why the waves would obey his voice. Do you understand what I am getting at? You see, that is why many, many people have trouble with prayer—because they think of what they are praying about as having no essential connection to God, at least none that makes any sense to them.

So we come now to look at this matter of our personal interaction with God with the purpose of redeeming our time and place in history. Ephesians 5:16 talks about "redeeming the time, because the days are evil" (KJV). Well, how are you going to redeem the time? What method do you have in mind? And the answer is by interacting with God where you are.

Jesus said, "You are the salt of the earth, . . . the light of the world" (Matt. 5:13–14). You, individually, are going through space and time, and there is absolutely no one else who is going to be moving through space and time where you are. You are going to have relationships to other people and things as you go through space and time, and your work is to show forth the grace and glory of God in that place where you are.

Now, people who have no relationship with God have to go through their place and time uprooted from God. They have no resources beyond their own strength and cleverness, which is why they behave the way that they do. There's a big fuss these days about ethics. That's not new. The Bible has some things to say about ethics, why people behave the way that they do—it's because they are uprooted from God. The biblical word for their condition is *corruption*. Corruption is what happens when you have a living thing that is uprooted from its life source. If you pull up a cabbage plant and leave it on the back porch for a few weeks, what will happen to it? It will die and decompose and, if you leave it there long enough, it will even fall to pieces and become dust. That is corruption.

You are given a new life when you are born into the kingdom of the heavens. That life is an interactive life with God. You turn your mind and your feelings toward God. As Paul says, you set your affections on things above, not on things on this earth (Col. 3:2). He talks about the mind of the Spirit in Colossians 3 and Romans 8, and sowing to the flesh and to the Spirit in Galatians 6. One who "sows to [the] flesh" will reap what? "Corruption" (6:8). Why? Because the flesh on its own naturally dies. It is meant to live in union with God; we are meant to be inhabited by God. You who sow to the Spirit will reap everlasting life. That kind of life doesn't fall prey to corruption; it just keeps going.

LIVING IN THE
TWENTY-THIRD PSALM

The "praying and saying" verses we are going to look at on Jesus's praying might be a little upsetting. These verses, and others like them, work like hand grenades that preachers just lob out in the audience, and everyone runs for cover. I hope you will be willing to bear the tension. After all, learning to live in the kingdom of the heavens is something that is often tense and embarrassing. One of the things you will notice in the passages is that the disciples were often embarrassed because they tried to do things and couldn't. Or they were shocked by what Jesus did in such a casual manner. Faith is often expressed by the casual manner in which people act. The expression of their faith has an everyday feel about it.

An old preacher once said, "If your stuff is thin, you will have to holler loud to make it thick." A lot of hollering goes on because people's faith is weak. In the story of Elijah and the four hundred prophets of Baal on Mt. Carmel, after the prophets had wailed all morning for Baal to respond, Elijah told them, "Holler a little louder! Maybe he is meditating, or has gone on a journey, or possibly he is asleep. Holler a little louder!" (1 Kings 18:27, paraphrase). So, no hollering for us.

Casualness shows the confidence of our interaction with the rule of God from the heavens here and now.

Casual confidence is what we see in passages such as Psalm 23. We need to take passages like this and meditate on them as something for our real life. "The Lord is my shepherd, I shall not want." Stop there for a moment and think: You are going to go through this whole day without wanting. Obviously today is going to be different, isn't it? But after all, that is what it says. And we have other passages from the New Testament: "My God will fully satisfy every need of yours according to his riches in glory in Christ Jesus" (Phil. 4:19). Is that real, or shall we just make another song out of those pretty words? "My God will fully satisfy all my needs." So now you have that in your head, but what is in your heart and in your life?

My aim in this chapter is to get you to concentrate on that question for yourselves as Christians. I want you to have confidence in the constant interaction that says, "Because of my experience, because it is reality, 'The Lord is my shepherd, I shall not want. He makes me lie down in green pastures; he leads me beside still waters; he restores my soul. He leads me in right paths for his name's sake. Even though I walk through the darkest valley, I fear no evil.'" Today you are not going to fear any evil. This is going to be another new day. "I fear no evil, for you are with me." Don't you suppose that that is something we would *know*, something we would know because of the presence of God actually making a difference in our lives as we trust him? "Your rod and your staff—they comfort me." Rods and staffs, that sounds like experience doesn't it? "You prepare a table before me in the presence of my enemies; you anoint my head with oil; my cup overflows. Surely goodness and mercy shall follow me all the days of my life, and I shall dwell in the house of the Lord my whole life long."

Psalm 23 was not written so that we could recite it at funerals. One of our problems as a church is that so many of the wonderful statements in the scriptures that are meant to reflect the honest experiences of those who have learned to live in interaction with God are in fact ritualistically and magically quoted by people who don't believe a bit of it, because they are scared to death! Nothing has ever happened to them that they are certain is the personal hand of God in their lives. And it drains the life out of those verses. Take Psalm 23 into the day with you tomorrow. It is the presence of the Lord with us.

Consider this passage from Hebrews 13:5–6:

> For he has said, "I will never leave you or forsake you."
> So we can say with confidence, "The Lord is my helper;
> I will not be afraid. What can anyone do to me?"

God's presence is the whole story. *This interaction between us and the God who is present with us always is what the resurrection is really about.* The meaning of the resurrection isn't just that Jesus won; it's that *he is now living with us.* So how does that work? It works with words. The kingdom of God works with words. Remember, we are talking about a reality that is personal through and through. That chair you are sitting on, and all of the other things we are trained so carefully to believe are independent, are not going along on their own. They are all subject constantly to the will and word of God. That's faith! That's 23rd Psalm faith.

When Paul says things like, "I know the one in whom I have put my trust, and I am sure that he is able to guard until that day what I have entrusted to him" (2 Tim. 1:12), he is talking on the basis of experience. And that experience came about as a result of the encounter between himself and God and the daily knowledge of God's hand in his life.

PRAYING AND SAYING

Praying and *saying* are two categories of words that we speak that can be represented by the following New Testament stories. Matthew 8:5–13 shows us a case where someone observed Jesus at work and recognized something about him. As we go through these verses, try to formulate in your own mind what it is he recognized.

> When he entered Capernaum, a centurion [a Roman officer] came to him, appealing to him and saying, "Lord, my servant is lying at home paralyzed, in terrible distress." And he said to him, "I will come and cure him." (vv. 5–7)

Jesus knows that we are living in a universe in which that makes perfectly good sense. If there is some disorder, it can be fixed. So he is working, and he will go with the Father and do that.

> The centurion answered, "Lord, I am not worthy to have you come under my roof; but only speak the word." (v. 8)

"Only speak the word." This is a personal kingdom, and this man knows the power of words.

"Speak the word, and my servant will be healed. For I also am a man under authority." (v. 8)

That's the key. This man had experience with words spoken with authority. Because he had authority, the centurion could say to the soldiers under him, "Go," and they would go (v. 9). But what if just anyone off the street came in and told a soldier to go? What would happen? Nothing! Or the fellow might find himself in some kind of trouble. The centurion knew what it was to be in command, to give orders and see them have an immediate effect. He had watched Jesus speak words and had seen their similar effect; things *happened* as a result. This is how things work in a personal kingdom.

There is nothing magic in words, but there is power in them when they fit into the kingdom. Watch what Jesus says to the centurion after he hears his analogy (v. 9), which is essentially a testament to Jesus's authority. He turns around as if to say, "Listen, folks, I want you to observe what this man has just done." Jesus is talking to his disciples there. He is not talking to Romans, but to Jews—*Jews who are supposed to know* about the kingdom of God—and he says something pretty discouraging to them:

> In no one in Israel have I found such faith. I tell you, many will come from east and west and will eat with Abraham and Isaac and Jacob in the kingdom of heaven, while the heirs of the kingdom [as it existed up until Jesus's time] will be thrown into the outer darkness. (vv. 10–12)

Well, that was enough to get him hanged right there. But you see Jesus was talking about faith; he knew the teaching of

Isaiah and used it himself: "This people honors me with their lips, but their hearts are far from me" (Matt. 15:8). It is very sad to see this among people who in a certain way are earnest Christians, and they speak the words, but the fact of the matter is that their hearts are turned toward everything else but God. I don't mean to offend anyone, but you have to understand that faith is something that involves the focus of the heart on God. You can see how that works in this case.

THE FATE OF THE FIG TREE

Another good example of praying and saying is in Mark 11:12–14, 20–24. This was closer to the time of Jesus's crucifixion, and he was going into Jerusalem from Bethany:

> Seeing in the distance a fig tree in leaf, he went to see whether perhaps he would find anything on it. When he came to it, he found nothing but leaves. . . . He said to it, "May no one ever eat fruit from you again." And his disciples heard it. (vv. 13–14)

(The philosopher Bertrand Russell used this story to say that Jesus was really a bad person—short tempered and angry, the kind of man who would just say, "Curse that tree!" But I understand that this was the sort of tree that should have had figs on it when it had leaves, so let's get past that and not get hung up on it.)

When they were heading back into Jerusalem the next morning, they saw the fig tree "withered away to its roots" (v. 20).

It wasn't just dead, it was dried up from the roots. It was dead wood, it was dried wood, it was withered wood. Remember, this is a personal universe, and that fig tree is held together by the personal will and act of God. It responds to language authoritatively spoken. Jesus didn't have to say to Peter, "Go back to Mary and Martha's house and get the chain saw. Let's take this tree out!"

After they saw what happened to the tree, Jesus told his disciples:

> Have faith in God. Truly I tell you, if you say to this mountain, "Be taken up and thrown into the sea," and if you do not doubt in your heart, but believe that what you say will come to pass, it will be done for you. So I tell you, whatever you ask for in prayer, believe that you have received it, and it will be yours. (vv. 22–24)

One of the good things about this passage is that it uses both saying and praying in such a way that you understand that we are talking about the same thing. Praying and saying constitute a continuum.

WHEN TO PRAY AND
WHEN TO SAY

If you look at Mark 9:14–29, you will see that sometimes it is appropriate to pray and sometimes it is appropriate to say. This is the story about the possessed boy who was brought to the disciples while Jesus was on the Mount of Transfiguration. When Jesus returned, the boy's father told him that his disciples were unable to cast out the demon. Jesus said, "You faithless generation," faithless babies, "how much longer must I be among you?" (v. 19) and then he cast out the demon. But later,

> When he had entered the house, his disciples asked him privately, "Why could we not cast it out?" He said to them, "This kind can come out only through prayer and fasting." (vv. 28–29)

But he didn't pray and fast at the time, did he? He was all caught up.

You see, in praying we are not just addressing God and asking him to dump something over here or over there; we are involved in a relationship with the thing we are praying about. We are *willing* that God's will be done upon earth, and we are speaking to God about it. When we are empowered to live in his name, we may speak to that in dependence upon God. Either way, it is the same triangle. And depending on where our confidence and authority are, we will go to praying or we will go to saying. Saying and praying.

POWER IN THE NAME

I want to be sure that you understand the key phrase "in Jesus's name" and have plenty of illustrations from scripture dealing with it. Jesus told his disciples in John 16:

If you ask anything of the Father in my name, he will give it to you. Until now you have not asked for anything in my name. Ask and you will receive, so that your joy may be complete. (vv. 23–24)

He had previously told them in John 15, as he talked about their being branches abiding in him as the vine:

If you abide in me, and my words abide in you, ask for whatever you wish, and it will be done for you. (v. 7)

Jesus was introducing a way of behaving within the structure of the kingdom.

Let's look at how Peter and John lived this out in Acts 3:1–10. In this story, we see them going up to the temple to pray. It is a good place to be going. In verse 2 we learn about a lame fellow whose job was to sit by the gate called Beautiful and beg for alms, and in verse 3 he was doing his job. Seeing Peter and John about to go into the temple, he asked them for alms. In response, Peter and John both fastened their eyes on him—all of the details here are interesting and important—verse 4 says, "Peter looked intently at him, as did John." They both locked on to this guy. They really got personal. This is crucial to working in the kingdom of heaven. Many people cannot do much in this area, because they have not come to the point where they can really connect with people. They are too frightened, insecure, or hostile or there's something within them that won't allow them to be loving enough.

Peter said, "Look at us." So now we have the two-way street going here—this is real personal contact. And then Peter said:

I have no silver or gold, but what I have I give you . . . (v. 6)

Do you suppose that Peter actually already *had* something? He *thought* he had something, didn't he? He thought he had it right there. Do you suppose that translates into experience? Where was it, do you suppose? It was in his body. Have you heard that your body is a temple of the Holy Spirit? Do you suppose that *means* something, or are those more nice words that belong in a song?

Peter *knew* he had something. He felt in his pocket (Did they have pockets in those days? Toga pockets?), and there was no silver or gold. But he knew that he had *something*. And did he *ever* have something! Clearly, he had learned this from Jesus.

But what I have I give you; in the name of Jesus Christ of Nazareth . . . (v. 6)

Why did he say that? Because that's his *authority*. Authority is in the name.

Peter's gift? "Stand up and walk" (v. 6). But Peter wasn't done with him; I mean, this got really embarrassing. Keep watching the details. Peter grabbed the lame man and jerked him up (v. 7). One of the things you will notice if you study the New Testament realistically—looking for the psychology, the culture, the sociology, the human events that are going on there—is that in nearly all of the miracles somebody did something. They didn't just sort of stand there and wait for God to act before they would show their hand. You know why that is? That is because they had faith. And they were willing to put themselves on the line. Peter put himself on the line:

He took him by the right hand and raised him up; and immediately his feet and ankles were made strong. (v. 7)

THE ULTIMATE APOLOGETIC

The ultimate apologetic—that is to say, the ultimate lifter of doubt—is the believer acting in faith in an interactive life with God. That's it. *People need to see individuals living in daily interaction with the kingdom of the heavens:* praying and saying. If we want to really attack doubt, what we have to attack is our own hesitancy to step up. And don't respond to that by saying, "But I am afraid I will be made a fool!" The biggest fools are those who do nothing, because they are afraid they will be seen as fools. And of course, that just testifies to their faith. The disciples were willing at least to be fools, weren't they? They got out there on a limb, sawed it off, and hit the ground, and they didn't even have to *try* to memorize that lesson. They knew it without memorizing it. That is what life does. Pain is a great teacher.

The most important thing for us to do by way of apologetics is to teach in such a way that people who do not really have confidence in the genuine interaction of the individual with the Great Shepherd will be led to make sense of it and will be inspired to experiment; that is, they will *try something.* This is where God will meet them. And when it happens, they ought to be dissuaded from saying, "Oh, it was a coincidence." But God wants to know how badly they want him. When some people take a step or two and God meets them, they call it a "coincidence," and their faith never gets off the ground. Why do they say that? Because they don't want to appear stupid; they don't want to appear gullible.

Abraham, the man of faith, went out not knowing where he was going. That was not a blind leap of faith, because Abraham knew God. He *knew* God. He didn't know where he was going, but he knew he was going with God. That is what our knowledge of the kingdom does. When we share these thoughts with other believers, it may open their minds to a new dimension of faith and hope, vision and work, as they read now with new eyes such words as these from the above scriptures and see the manner of life in the kingdom of God. It enables us to step out in faith and then to invite others to join us.

The first step for those desiring to enter God's family is the obvious one of recognizing that an act of entry is necessary; they are currently not members of it. And none can enter the family of God under the pretense that they have a right to be there. All enter, if they enter at all, *Dei gratia,* by the graciousness of the head of the family, God the Father. There are no exceptions to this rule. So a deep humbling is a prerequisite for entry. But to enter is to enter into life, for those who enter find at last what it is to be loved and to be filled with love—not with sentiment, but love—for all people, regardless of whether they too are members of God's family or not. Love, like other attitudes and virtues, cannot be taught. It can only be caught. You can teach people that they *ought* to love, but not *to love*. But when people enter the family of God, they are in a position to catch the divine diseases of love, patience, gentleness, and so on.

And once people are inside this family, they can see a lot of things they never saw before. They are likely to find that they have spent a great deal of time running away from certain unpleasant facts about themselves, above all from the fact that it was altogether absurd for them to crave and demand that others love them. Other things they discover are that many of their disappointments and trials were for their own good and that other disappointments were due to their own blundering about.

We must help others all the way through this process in a way that goes beyond traditional apologetics—presenting arguments responding to presupposed objections. We must adopt a teaching posture that presupposes inquiry to arrive at knowledge and the will to communicate, a posture of joint discovery and of understanding *together*. These are natural and essential parts of living in community with others. So maintain a teaching posture as you go, and work with those around you in the gentle manner of Jesus. If you do, it will indeed be a service to all to carry out the work of apologetics.

Gracious Lord, we are thankful to be drawn into your kingdom. We are thankful, wherever we are in our work, in our family, in our play, or whatever else may be happening, to know that we are under your kingdom rule, that heaven is over us, and that our God reigns. Lord, help us to be simple, humble, and thoughtful as we listen to others and help them come to faith in the One who has given us life. In Jesus's name we pray. Amen.

ACKNOWLEDGMENTS

There are many people to thank and acknowledge in the writing of this book. Let me begin by thanking the staff and members of Grace Church, who invited a humble philosopher to come and talk with them about Christian apologetics. I am grateful to my father for his guidance and support in bringing these words to print so a much broader audience could benefit from them.

Many thanks to Jane Willard, Michael Maudlin, Bill Heatley, and Larissa Heatley for their steadfast encouragement and patience throughout the many ups and downs of bringing this book into being. I am grateful for the work of Alexander Lamascus, who helped transcribe some of the talks, and for the skill and insight of my editors, Michael Maudlin and Elsa Dixon.

Several of Dallas's friends and former students advised me along the way, particularly J. P. Moreland, Joe Gorra, and Bill Heatley. Frank Pastore and John Ortberg contributed by doing what they do naturally—asking Dallas really good questions.

I am eternally grateful to my parents for the profound Christian faith and heritage that they lived and passed on to me. And I am thankful for the love and prayers of my Bible Study family who hold me, my family, and our efforts before the throne of God with such faithfulness.

Most of all, *thanks be to God for his unspeakable gift!*

—*RWH*

NOTES

INTRODUCTION

1. Parts of this Introduction were originally published as Dallas Willard's "Apologetics in the Manner of Jesus," *Facts for Faith* (Reasons to Believe, 1999); www.reasons.org.

2. This Greek word for "humility" includes the idea of having a humble opinion of oneself, a deep sense of one's moral littleness, modesty, humility, and lowliness of mind.

CHAPTER ONE

1. "The heavens," in plural, most accurately portrays the direct presence of God to those who trust and serve him. Nothing—no human being or institution, no time, no space, no spiritual being, no event—stands between God and those who trust him. The "heavens" are always there with you no matter what, and the "first heaven," in biblical terms, is precisely the atmosphere or air that surrounds your body . . . the space immediately around us from which God watches and acts. See a more complete discussion of this phrase in *The Divine Conspiracy: Rediscovering Our Hidden Life in God* (San Francisco: HarperSanFrancisco, 1998), pp. 67–68.

2. Jane Wagner, *The Search for Signs of Intelligent Life in the Universe,* rev. ed. (New York: Harper Perennial, 1991), p. 18.

3. Willard, *The Divine Conspiracy;* and my *Renovation of the Heart: Putting on the Character of Christ* (Colorado Springs: NavPress, 2002).

CHAPTER TWO

1. Richard Robinson, *An Atheist's Values* (Oxford: Clarendon, 1964), p. 120.

2. See J. P. Moreland, *Love Your God with All Your Mind: The Role of Reason in the Life of the Soul,* rev. ed. (Colorado Springs: NavPress, 2012).

CHAPTER THREE

1. John Stott, *Your Mind Matters* (Downers Grove, IL: InterVarsity, 2006), p. 37.

2. Stott, *Your Mind Matters*, p. 38, quoting D. Martyn Lloyd-Jones, *Studies in the Sermon on the Mount* (Grand Rapids, MI: Eerdmans, 1960), pp. 129–30.

3. Joseph Glanvill (1636–80), quoted in Andrew Martin Fairbairn, *The Philosophy of the Christian Religion* (London: Hodder and Stoughton, 1903), p. ii.

4. A Bessemer converter is a large pear-shaped container used in the manufacturing of steel from iron. The key principle is removal of impurities from the iron by oxidation with air being blown through the molten iron. The oxidation also raises the temperature of the iron mass and keeps it molten.

5. A. B. Bruce, *Apologetics, or Christianity Defensively Stated,* 3rd ed. (Edinburgh: International Theological Library, 1905), p. 37.

6. Charles Finney, *Revival Lectures* (Old Tappan, NJ: Revell, n.d.), p. 201.

CHAPTER FOUR

1. Epictetus, *Works,* Carter-Higginson translation, abridged, bk. 1, chap. 16.

2. George Fox, *The Journal of George Fox,* Everyman's Library (London: Dent, 1948), p. 15.

3. C. S. Lewis, *The Abolition of Man* (London: Oxford Univ. Press, 1943).

4. I discuss the issue of hell and how one arrives there in greater detail in my *Renovation of the Heart: Putting on the Character of Christ* (Colorado Springs: NavPress, 2002), chap. 3.

5. C. S. Lewis, *The Great Divorce* (San Francisco: HarperOne, 2009), p. 75.

6. A. E. Wilder-Smith, *He Who Thinks Has to Believe* (Green Forest, AR: New Leaf, 1982).

7. J. L. Mackie, *The Miracle of Theism: Arguments for and Against the Existence of God* (New York: Oxford Univ. Press, 1982).

8. Arthur Koestler, *The Sleepwalkers: A History of Man's Changing Vision of the Universe* (London: Penguin, 1990).

9. Harry Emerson Fosdick, *Great Voices of the Reformation: An Anthology* (New York: Random House, 1952), p. 122.

CHAPTER FIVE

1. There is also such a thing as a deductive or analogical proof. If you hold the standard of logical implication or entailment of premises to conclusion, nearly every argument we use in the course of life will prove to be invalid. Then we will say it is not a proof. The next step is (if you are inclined, and I don't know what your epistemological inclinations are) to say that we don't know the conclusion to be true. This means that the conclusion would be false and the premises true. But certainly nearly everything we count as knowledge does not fall under that kind of strict requirement. I mentioned the buildings downtown because that is obviously a case where people are quite good at getting the true conclusion from their premises. And all we want to do here in religion is apply the same kinds of standards to our subject matter as people would apply to subject matter generally. So if you were to go into the details of this argument, like any analogical or inductive argument, you would question whether or not the premises are indeed the sort of premises that make that conclusion reasonable in other cases. It isn't as if this were beyond reproach, but that is the way you would do it.

2. Words by Thomas O. Chisholm, music by William M. Runyan, 1923.

3. "Break Thou the Bread of Life," words by Mary A. Lathbury, music by William F. Sherwin, 1877.

4. In particular, F. F. Bruce's *The New Testament Documents: Are They Reliable?* (Grand Rapids, MI: Eerdmans, 2003); and his *The Defense of the Gospel in the New Testament* (Grand Rapids, MI: Eerdmans, 1981).

5. R. C. Sproul, John Gerstner, and Arthur Lindsley, *Classical Apologetics* (Grand Rapids, MI: Zondervan, 1984).

CHAPTER SIX

1. C. S. Lewis, in *The Problem of Pain* (San Francisco: HarperOne, 2001), provides a wonderful treatment of the role and place of pain in our world.

2. An argument is judged from two perspectives: (1) When it comes to form, does the argument have all the right parts (premises and conclusion)? (A formally valid argument means the form is correct.) (2) Are the contents of the premises themselves true?

3. Aldous Huxley, *Brave New World* (Garden City, NY: Doubleday, 1932), chap. 17.

4. Of course, childbirth is the primary example of how this is true, but there are others: training of all kinds (e.g., athletic, musical, artistic, academic), medical procedures, vocational duties (e.g., fire fighters, soldiers, police, medical personnel). "Unto This Last" (*Cornhill Magazine,* December 1860), by John Ruskin, gives a clear picture of the due occasion of key professions that maintain the goods of society.

5. Jeremy Bentham, *Introduction to the Principles of Morals and Legislation* (Oxford: Clarendon, 1907), p. 1.

6. Omar Khayyám, *Rubáiyát of Omar Khayyám: The Astronomer-Poet of Persia,* trans. Edward FitzGerald (New York: Crowell, 1921), quatrain 99.

7. C. S. Lewis, *The Weight of Glory* (San Francisco: HarperOne, 2001), p. 15.

8. Thomas Moore, "Come, Ye Disconsolate," *Sacred Songs,* 1816.

9. David Hume, *Dialogues Concerning Natural Religion* (London: Blackwood and Sons, 1907), p. 134: "Is he willing to prevent evil, but not able? Then he is impotent. Is he able, but not willing? Then he is malevolent. Is he both able and willing? Whence then is evil?"

10. Contempt is a product of anger that has settled in and causes us to think of someone in such a degrading way that we don't even see them as human anymore.

11. For a further treatment of dealing with desire, see my "The Spirit Is Willing: The Body As a Tool for Spiritual Growth," in *Christian Educator's Handbook on Spiritual Formation,* ed. Kenneth Gangel and James Wilhoit (Grand Rapids, MI: Baker, 1994); my "Beyond Pornography: Spiritual Formation Studied in a Particular Case" (paper presented at the Talbot School of Theology's "Christian Spirituality and Soul Care" conference in September 2008); and my *Renovation of the Heart: Putting on the Character of Christ* (Colorado Springs: NavPress, 2002).

12. Francis Thompson, "The Hound of Heaven," in D. H. S. Nicholson and A. H. E. Lee, eds., *The Oxford Book of English Mystical Verse* (Oxford: Clarendon, 1917), #239.

CHAPTER SEVEN

1. "In the Garden," Charles A. Miles, 1913.

2. Frederick B. Meyer, *The Secret of Guidance* (Chicago: Moody, 2010), pp. 28–29.

3. Dallas Willard, *Hearing God: Developing a Conversational Relationship with God* (Downers Grove, IL: InterVarsity, 1999).

RESOURCES FOR
FURTHER STUDY

BOOKS

Augustine of Hippo. *The City of God.* Many editions. Written in the early
  fifth century to explain Christianity in relation to competing religions and
  philosophies.

Greg L. Bahnsen. "Socrates or Christ: The Reformation of Christian
  Apologetics." In Gary North, ed., *Foundations of Christian Scholarship.*
  Portland, OR: Ross House, 1976. Pp. 191–239.

A. B. Bruce. *Apologetics, or Christianity Defensively Stated.* Edinburgh:
  Clark, 1905. The introduction includes excellent statements about what
  apologetics is.

L. Russ Bush, ed. *Classical Readings in Christian Apologetics: A.D. 100–1800.*
  Grand Rapids, MI: Academie, 1983.

Joseph Butler. *The Analogy of Religion to the Constitution and Course of Nature.*
  London: Horsfield, 1765. Joseph Butler was an Anglican bishop and one
  of the great apologetes of the Christian church. His book shows that if
  we merely apply the standards of reasoning that we apply to everything
  else to the area of religion, the truths of the Christian faith will stand up
  under that test, and we will come to the knowledge of God. A great critic
  of that reasoning is David Hume, who wrote *Dialogues Concerning Natural
  Religion* (1779). If you are really interested in getting into both sides of the
  argument, you might want to look at both.

E. J. Carnell. *An Introduction to Christian Apologetics.* Grand Rapids, MI:
  Eerdmans, 1948.

Irving M. Copi. *Introduction to Logic.* Many editions, but get an older edition if
  possible. A good introduction to the basic concepts of logic.

William Lane Craig. *Reasonable Faith: Christian Truth and Apologetics.* 3rd ed.
  Wheaton, IL: Crossway, 2008.

Norman L. Geisler. *Christian Apologetics.* Grand Rapids, MI: Baker, 1976.

Étienne Gilson. *History of Christian Philosophy in the Middle Ages.* New York: Random House, 1955. Especially parts 1 and 2.

Timothy Keller. *The Reason for God: Belief in an Age of Skepticism.* New York: Penguin, 2008. A good contemporary treatment of many very important topics. I particularly recommend the introduction and chapters 1, 2, and 9.

C. S. Lewis. I suggest that you read everything by C. S. Lewis, but for the specific purposes of our efforts in apologetics, I highly recommend *Mere Christianity, The Problem of Pain, The Screwtape Letters,* and *God in the Dock.* Many editions of all are available.

James D. Martin. *The Reliability of the Gospels.* London: Hodder & Stoughton, 1959. A good treatment of, as the title says, the reliability of the gospels.

John Montgomery. *Faith Founded on Fact: Essays in Evidential Apologetics.* Nashville: Thomas Nelson, 1978.

J. P. Moreland. As with Lewis, you would do well to read all of Moreland's work, but particularly *Love Your God with All Your Mind: The Role of Reason in the Life of the Soul.* Colorado Springs: NavPress, 2012; *Does God Exist?: The Debate Between Theists and Atheists.* With Kai Nelson. Amherst, NY: Prometheus, 1993; and *Scaling the Secular City.* Grand Rapids, MI: Baker, 1987.

Max Picard. *The Flight from God.* Washington, DC: Regnery, 1951. This penetrating little book of some years back describes what has now become the predominant form of Western life. God and his commands could be automatically assumed in most social contexts forty years ago, but now secularity is assumed.

John Polkinghorne. *The Polkinghorne Reader: Science, Faith, and the Search for Meaning.* Edited by Thomas Jay Oord. West Conshohocken, PA: Templeton, 2010. A valuable collection of writings from a top "scientist-theologian." Topics covered include evil, the nature of science, the physical world, human nature, creation, and time.

Bernard Ramm. *Varieties of Christian Apologetics.* Grand Rapids, MI: Baker, 1961.

J. K. S. Reid. *Christian Apologetics.* Grand Rapids, MI: Eerdmans, 1970.

Jean-François Revel. *The Flight from Truth.* New York: Random House, 1991. A study of how deceit has been the controlling structure of twentieth-century existence.

Bertrand Russell. *Why I Am Not a Christian, and Other Essays on Religion and Related Subjects.* New York: Simon & Schuster, 1957.

Patrick Sherry. *Spirit, Saints, and Immortality.* Albany: State Univ. of New York Press, 1984. The significant points in the book are the existence of saintly people as a fundamental datum of apologetics, though Sherry does not often use that word, involving four main subcomponents: the Spirit of God, saintliness, likeness to God, and immortality (life to come).

R. C. Sproul, John Gerstner, and Arthur Lindsley. *Classical Apologetics: A Rational Defense of the Christian Faith and a Critique of Presuppositional Apologetics.* Grand Rapids, MI: Academie, 1984. See my comments in Chapter 5.

John R. W. Stott. *Your Mind Matters to God.* Downers Grove, IL: InterVarsity, 1972. A very small book (61 pages) showing how faith and thought belong together.

Elton Trueblood. *A Place to Stand: A Practical Guide to Christian Faith as a Solid Point from Which to Operate in Contemporary Living.* New York: Harper & Row, 1969.

Cornelius Van Til. *The Defense of the Faith.* Phillipsburg, NJ: Presbyterian and Reformed, 1980. Especially chapters 5–7.

Dallas Willard. *Knowing Christ Today: Why We Can Trust Spiritual Knowledge.* San Francisco: HarperOne, 2009.

WEBSITES

www.dwillard.org. Many of Dr. Willard's free articles and other resources, including an apologetics glossary to accompany this book.

www.reasonablefaith.org. Provides an intelligent, articulate, and uncompromising yet gracious Christian perspective on important issues concerning the truth of the Christian faith. Features the work of William Lane Craig.

www.reasons.org. A valuable resource in the discussion of how scientific research consistently supports the truth of the Bible and faith in God. Normally up-to-date with the latest findings.

SPIRITUAL DISCIPLINES AND DISCIPLESHIP

Richard Foster. *Celebration of Discipline: The Path to Spiritual Growth.* San Francisco: HarperSanFrancisco, 1978.

John Ortberg. *The Life You've Always Wanted: Spiritual Disciplines for Ordinary People.* Grand Rapids, MI: Zondervan, 2002. A good introduction for those just getting started with spiritual disciplines.

Dallas Willard. *The Spirit of the Disciplines: Understanding How God Changes Lives.* San Francisco: Harper & Row, 1988.

SCRIPTURE INDEX

SUBJECT INDEX

Abolition of Man (Lewis), 64
Abraham: children of, 104; as a
    "friend" of God, 97–99; as man of
    faith, 169; sending his servant to
    find wife for Isaac, 148
abstinence, 22
Achan's story, 102–3
action. *See* human action
Adam and Eve story, 50–51, 66–67
All in the Family (TV show), 28
analogy: analogical reasoning of, 89;
    of God as creator of humanity
creation, 87, 88–90
animal sacrifice, 100–102
Apologetics (Bruce), 48
apologetic attitudes: being humble,
    generous, and open toward other
    people, 3, 52–53; confidence in
    God and his truth, 52; a true desire
    to lovingly serve, 53
apologetics: as act of loving our neigh-
    bor, 2–3; as an aid to faith, 48; as
    being for everyone, 33; the context
    of, 25, 29–32; examining the nature
    of biblical, 39–43; God's speaking
    to us issue of, 147; intellectual de-
    bates and arguments engaged in by,
    1–2; moving away from argument
    toward real-life experience, 155; as
    a New Testament helping ministry
    requiring thinking and reasoning,
    2, 9–10; origins and definition of, 1;

the ultimate, 168–70; understand-
    ing what it is not, 46–52
apologetic work: happiness through, 34,
    35; intellectual bullying as contrary
    to, 49–50; for joint discovery and
    understanding of together, 169–70;
    "making sense" of Christian faith,
    85–87; problem of the existence of
    evil in, 91; role of reason in, 44–46;
    the scope of, 25; the spirit of, 16–17;
    three types of Christian attitude
    required for, 52–53
apologists: as characterized by "hum-
    bleness of mind," 3; as disciples of
    Jesus, 2; the four Gospels written
    by, 2; gentleness and reverence of
    communication by, 4–5, 33–34,
    50; living out of the kingdom of
    God resources, 143–46; as relent-
    less servants of truth, 3–4. *See also*
    Christians; disciples
"appropriate basis," 13–14
atheism, 74
An Atheist's Values (Robinson), 28
authority: to act on your knowledge,
    15; of the name of Jesus Christ,
    161–63, 166–68; what we know
    by, 13

Beatitudes, 30
beliefs: comparing knowledge to
    knowledge and faith, 12; distin-

beliefs *(continued)*
  guishing commitment from, 13;
  in God, 61–64; listening to both
  doubt and, 27. *See also* doubt; idea
  systems
Bentham, Jeremy, 117–18
Bezalel, 59
Bible: New Testament: apologetics as
  a ministry of the, 2, 9–10; on communication between humanity and
  God, 83; having a personal walk
  with God presupposition of the
  teachings of, 146; Martin Luther's
  commentary on Romans, 81–82;
  the psychology of the, 167; seeking
  God through the, 106
Bible: Old Testament: book of Job, 111,
  130; as highest iteration of God
  given to humanity, 99; the images
  of God in the, 69; laws of corporate responsibility from the, 102–3;
  predictions on the Jewish people
  in the, 105; on seeing the kingdom
  of the heavens, 59; seeking God
  through the, 105–6, 109; story of
  Achan in the, 102–3; unique nature
  of the, 99–100
Bible: as the best-attested record of
  the ancient world, 107–8; comparing what we hear from God to
  scriptures of the, 154–55; the images of God in the, 69; mistrans-
  lation and misuse of scriptures in
  the, 104–5, 106–7; "reconciliation"
  of science and the, 80; reliability of
  the, 108–9; on seeing the kingdom
  of the heavens, 59; seeking God
  through the, 105–9; tracing the
  relationship of God and Abraham,
  97–99
biblegateway.com, 12
biblical Christians, 106
big-bang theory, 75

body: as independent power source,
  89; resurrection of Jesus's, 143–44,
  160. *See also* humanity
book of Job, 111, 130
Brave New World (Huxley), 116
Bruce, A. B., 48
Bunker, Archie (*All in the Family*
  character), 28

Calvin, John, 69
Campus Crusade, 144
Candide (Voltaire), 134
centurion's faith story, 161–63
"Christian evidences," 51
Christian gospel: doubt within the
  church as the greatest problem facing the, 25; perceived as truth, 19
Christianity: apologetics defined as
  vindication of, 49; "Christian
  evidences" to show truth of, 51;
  on God's benevolence and power,
  114–16; idea system that it is just
  superstition, 12; "making sense"
  of Christian faith and, 85–87;
  problem of evil and pain argument
  against, 113–22; understood as the
  discipline of Christ and the true
  humanism, 137
Christians: being a biblical, 106;
  organizations who debate on
  college campuses with, 143–44; the
  response to the problem of evil
  and pain argument by, 129–33; who
  believe that their faith is a superstition, 12. *See also* apologists
Classical Apologetics (Sproul, Gerstner,
  and Lindsley), 107
commitment vs. belief, 13
confidence in God, 52
corporate responsibility, 102–3
corruption, 157–58
cosmic evolution theory, 75–76
covenant with Abraham, 98–99

covetous person, 63

creation: Adam and Eve story on the, 50–51, 66–67; analogy of God as the creator of, 87, 88–90; for good, 89; Paul on the creation and the end of, 78; the process of, 88–90; series of causation for physical world, 72–74; a society of the redeemed as the crown jewel of, 96; understanding the power of the, 77. *See also* God; the physical world

cultural beliefs: about the nature of faith, 29; on doubt as being smart, 27

David, 58

defending the faith, 47, 49

Dei gratia (graciousness of God), 169

desire to serve, 53

desire vs. love, 115

disciples, 2. *See also* apologists

discipleship: correcting our ideas through experience of, 20; importance of ideas and role of, 22; meaning and spiritual life in, 21–22

The Divine Conspiracy (Willard), 20

double-mindedness, 15

doubt: dealing honestly with our, 29; on the existence of God, 61; Jesus's method with Thomas and his, 26–27; knowledge to eliminate, 15; listening to both beliefs and, 27; as problem within the church, 25; removed through submission to the Holy Spirit, 39; terrible and painful nature of, 50–51; the ultimate apologetic or lifter of, 168–70. *See also* beliefs

Elijah, 158

$E = mc^2$, 77, 79

energy: interrelationship of mass and, 77–79; radiance as manifestation of energy, 101

engagement, 22

Epictetus, 61

ethics, 157. *See also* moral development

evil: classical argument over a good God that allows suffering, 121–22; consideration of God as being responsible for all, 120–21; existence of, 91; human responsibility for, 134; Jesus as our best guide in standing against, 136–38; Lord's Prayer on being delivered from, 94; moral character development by choosing good over, 125–27; the "other" problem of getting rid of, 135–36; scriptural view on God as guarding against, 92–93; understanding that there is no good without, 125; when people do, 90. *See also* problem of pain and evil

faith: apologetics as an aid to, 48; Archie Bunker's humorous definition of, 28; building your life on, 81–82; comparing knowledge to belief and, 12; contrasting sight and, 82; "defending the," 47, 49; description of, 9–10; Holy Spirit as working in, 82; how reason serves, 45–46, 59–60; idea system of knowledge being opposed to, 12; knowledge intended to go together with, 81–82; mistaking "coincidence" as barrier to, 168–69; the nature of, 28–29; putting us in touch with reality of kingdom of God, 86; saving versus damning, 10; story on centurion's, 161–63; the terrible teachings of our culture on, 29; of the twenty-third psalm, 160; the ultimate apologetic acting in, 168–70

fear: apologetic work done in good conscience and, 33–34; reverence as another word for, 34

fig tree parable, 163–64
Finney, Charles, 52–53
Fox, George, 63
free will/choice, 125–27
Freud, Sigmund, 99

Garden of Eden story, 50–51, 66–67
generosity, 52–53
gentleness: apologetic work performed
with reverence and, 4–5, 33–34,
50; when working with the Holy
Spirit, 50
Gerstner, John, 107
Glanvill, Joseph, 45–46
God: becoming a servant of, 53; Christ
as the human image of personality of, 137–38; classical argument
over suffering allowed by a good,
121–22; commandment to love, 48;
communication between humanity
and, 83; confidence in his truth,
52; consideration of whether he
is responsible for all evil, 120–21;
creator analogy of, 87, 88–90; *Dei
gratia* (graciousness of God) of,
169; devoting all of our human
powers to, 10; hell as separation
from, 67–70; his good purposes in
human history, 92–97, 109; how
people hide from, 11–12; *imago
Dei* (image of God), 138; involvement in science and technology,
80–81; Old Testament images of,
69; omniscience and omnipotence
of, 66–67; our interaction with,
156–58; our personal relationship
with, 46, 145, 148–49, 155–56;
prayer as way to work with, 52;
problem of evil and pain argument
used against, 113–29; reason as a
basis of responsibility and submission before, 45, 58–59; reason as a
gift from, 16; relationship between
Abraham and, 97–99; reverence and

fear of, 34; seeking him through
the Bible, 105–9; surrendering our
will to, 136; trusting, 42; wish for
a perfect world to be provided by,
123–24. *See also* creation; kingdom
of God
God's benevolence: as allowing people
to suffer as part of his, 119; Christianity on God's power and, 114–16;
reliance on his greatness, goodness,
and, 133
God's existence: Epictetus on reason
as sufficient to establish, 61; infinite and self-subsistent nature of,
73, 91; questioning the presence
of evil in context of, 91; question
of why God is not more obvious,
65–66; reason used to believe in,
61–64; "village atheist" trick to
disprove, 11
God's speaking to us: hearing God
speak, 147–50; as important
apologetic topic, 147; learning to
know the voice of God when,
150; objections about the idea of,
152–53; our interaction with God
in context of, 156–58; a personal
example of, 151–52; praying and
saying elements of, 161–65; reality
of a personal relationship with God
through, 155–56; testing what we
hear, 15–154; the "three lights" for
testing, 154–55; what the scriptures
say about, 158–61. *See also* Holy
Spirit; prayer
"good" people/environment: expectations that God provide a, 123–24;
understanding that evil is necessary
for, 125. *See also* humanity
Gospels: on the Samaritan woman at
the well, 10; on seeing the kingdom of the heavens, 59; written by
apologists, 1
gospel. *See* Christian gospel

grace, 47
Great Commission, 22

happiness, 34, 35
Hearing God (Willard), 154
hell: defined as separation from God,
    67; the reason for, 68–70; symbol-
    ism of, 67–68
He Who Thinks Has to Believe (Wilder-
    Smith), 70
hiding from God, 11–12
Hitler, Adolf, 127, 135
Holocaust, 135
Holy Spirit: apologetics is assisted by
    reliance on the, 9; gentleness and
    reverence when working with the,
    50; as God's speaking to us, 146;
    the mark of the, 86; as one of the
    "three lights," 154; reason used to
    seek truth through the, 60, 107; re-
    moving doubts through submission
    to the, 39; resisting corruption by
    listening to the, 157–58; as working
    in faith, 82. *See also* God's speaking
    to us
"The Hound of Heaven" (Thomp-
    son), 138–39
human action: importance of context
    of the, 127; importance of order to,
    127–28; moral character develop-
    ment through, 125–27
human history: allowing people to
    approach God, 103–4; applying rea-
    son to, 90–92; God's good purposes
    in, 92–97, 109; laying the founda-
    tion for Jesus to come, 144–45; the
    scriptures as best-attested record
    of the ancient world, 107–8; self-
    subsistent God as the creator of,
    73–74, 91
humanity: analogy of God as cre-
    ator to the creation of, 87, 88–90;
    apologetic attitude toward, 3,
    52–53; belief that God will re-

deem us from suffering, 132–33;
    character development through
    making good choices, 125–27;
    communication between God
    and, 83; given the opportunity for
    moral development, 130–31; God's
    speaking to, 147–65; Old Testament
    as highest iteration of God given
    to, 99; our interaction with God,
    156–58; redeemed and the crown
    jewel of creation, 96; suffering and
    the responsibility of, 134; wish for a
    "perfect world" by, 123–24. *See also*
    body; "good" people/environment;
    problem of evil and pain
"humbleness of mind," 3, 52–53
Hume, David, 99, 133
Huxley, Aldous, 116

idea systems: corrected through
    discipleship, 20; how people are
    at the mercy of their own, 17–18;
    that Christianity is just another
    superstition, 12; that knowledge
    is opposed to faith, 11–12. *See also*
    beliefs
idolatry, 63–64
ignorance, 40
imago Dei (image of God), 138
Ingersoll, Bob, 11
Inquisition, 135
intellectual bullying, 49–50
InterVarsity, 144
*Introduction to the Principles of Morals
    and Legislation* (Bentham), 117–18
Isaac, 148
Israelites: brought out of Egypt by
    God, 102, 104; story of Achan,
    102–3. *See also* Jewish people

Jericho, 102
Jesus Christ: authority of the words
    spoken by, 161–63, 166–68; his
    method with doubters, 26–27; as

Jesus Christ *(continued)*
the human image of God's personality, 137–38; on knowledge of scripture without living them, 106; learning to live like, 21–22; as our guide for taking a stand against evil, 136–38; power in closing prayer "in the name" of, 165–68; recognized as master of the cosmos, 3; reflections on the relationship of David to, 58; resurrection of, 143–44, 160; sanctified in our hearts, 4; story of the centurion and, 161–62; teaching with reason and knowledge of, 57–60; tested by the Pharisees and Sadducees, 45; work to enfold people into his kingdom, 69

Jewish culture: God's work accomplished within the, 102–4; the unique history of the, 99–100

Jewish people: animal sacrifice practice of the, 100–102; covenant with Abraham and his descendents, 98–99; scripture predictions on the, 105; unique culture of the, 99–100. *See also* Israelites

Khayyám, Omar, 123

kingdom of God: apologists living out of the resources of, 143–46; faith putting us in touch with reality of, 86; gratitude for being drawn into the, 170; Jesus's work to enfold people into the, 69; learning to live like Christ in the, 21–22; the scriptures on seeing the, 59. *See also* God

knowledge: "appropriate basis" of, 13–14; comparing to belief and faith, 12; definition of, 13; eliminating doubt with continuous engagement with subject, 15; examining what the scriptures have to say about, 12; faith intended

to go together with, 81–82; idea system of faith being opposed to, 11–12; Jesus's teaching with reason and, 57–60; scientific method considered as the only basis of, 14–15. *See also* reason

"Knowledge is power," 64
Koestler, Arthur, 80

Large Hadron Collider (Switzerland), 77–78
Lewis, C. S., 64, 68–69, 130–31
Lindsley, Arthur, 107
Lloyd-Jones, Martyn, 42, 43
Lord's Prayer, 94
love: desire versus, 115; entering God's family and feeling, 169
love our neighbor: apologetics as act of, 2–3; Great Commandment to, 48
Luther, Martin, 81–82

Mackie, J. L., 74
making good choices, 125–27
mass and energy interrelationship, 77–79
The Message, 106
Meyer, Frederick B., 154
The Miracle of Theism (Mackie), 74
moral development: action and the context of the action for, 127; making good choices required for, 125–27; opportunity given to humanity for, 130–31. *See also* ethics
Moses, 73, 153
Mussolini, Benito, 135

natural law, 122
New Testament. *See* Bible: New Testament
Nicodemus, 59

Old Testament. *See* Bible: Old Testament
omnipotence of God, 66

omniscience of God, 66–67
openness toward others, 52–53
order, 76–77

pain: classical argument over a good
God that allows, 121–22; consideration of the value of, 117–19; as
a great teacher, 168; responsibility
of human beings for suffering and,
134; separating evil from, 116–17;
three examples of when it is preferable, 117. *See also* problem of evil
and pain
Pangloss (*Candide* fictional character), 134
Paul: on the creation and end of creation, 78–79; on the good purposes
of God, 95; on knowing God, 70;
on purpose of suffering, 133; on
setting your affections toward God,
157–58; warning against philosophy
and vain deceit, 40
"perfect world": humanity's wish for
a, 123; the validity of expecting
God to provide a, 124. *See also* the
physical world
Peter: on the authority of Jesus Christ,
166–68; on the Holy Spirit, 60
Pharisees, 45
philosophies: apologetics defined as
vindication of Christianity against
other, 49; danger of vain deceit
and, 40–41
the physical world: creating order in,
76–77; $E=mc^2$ (energy and mass
interrelationship) in the, 77–79;
myths of big-bang and cosmic
evolution on, 75–76; series of
causation for, 72–74; study of
God's action in sustaining reality
of, 78–79; temptation to believe
that it is all that exists, 64, 70; why
there is more than the, 71–72. *See
also* creation; "perfect world"

prayer: examining the reason for,
51–52; on gratitude for being
drawn into the kingdom of God,
170; the Lord's Prayer, 94; a personal example of the power of, 151–52;
power in closing "in Jesus's name,"
165–68; praying and saying, 161–65;
as working with God, 52. *See also*
God's speaking to us
praying and saying: Fate of the Fig
Tree story on, 163–64; the scriptures on when to pray and when
to say, 164–65; what the scriptures
have to say about, 161–63
problem of evil and pain: as argument against Christianity, 113–22;
description of the, 91; dissolving
the dilemma of the, 128–29; human
responsibility for, 134; Job on the,
111, 130; Thompson's "The Hound
of Heaven" dialogue on, 138–39.
See also evil; humanity; pain
problem of evil and pain argument:
the Christian response to the,
129–33; consideration as a formally
valid argument, 114; rejection of
the, 119–20; sequence of issues used
in the, 113
problem of evil and pain argument
analysis: character development
through making good choices,
125–27; consideration of God's
benevolence and power, 114–16;
consideration of the value of pain,
117–19; considering the importance of order, 127–28; dissolving
the dilemma of presence of moral
evil, 128–29; examining the wish
for a "perfect world," 123–24; of
a good God that allows suffering,
121–22; rejection of the argument,
119–20; separating pain from evil,
116–17; understanding that there is
no good without evil, 125

133; responsibility of human beings for pain and, 134
"Superseded Scientific Theories" (Wikipedia), 14

technological advances, 80–81
terrorist attack, 126, 129
thinking: answering vain deceit with good, 41; apologetics as helping ministry requiring, 2, 9–10. *See also* reason
Thomas, 26–27
Thompson, Francis, 138–39
trusting God, 42
truth: apologists as relentless servants of, 3–4; "Christian evidences" to show truth of Christianity, 51; Christian gospel perceived as, 19; clarity of Christ's, 60; confidence in God and his, 52; ensuring that our

ideas are build upon, 18; the Holy Spirit guiding the reason that leads to, 60, 107; the nature of, 18–19 twenty-third psalm, 158–61

UCLA Medical Center, 151
the ultimate apologetic, 168–70

vain deceit and philosophy, 40–41
"village atheist" trick, 11
voice of God. *See* God's speaking to us
Voltaire, 134

Warren, Rick, 154
Wilder-Smith, A. E., 70
Willard, Dallas, 20, 22
World Trade Center terrorist attack, 129

Your Mind Matters (Stott), 42